JOHN DONNE

Sean Haldane

Greenwich Exchange, London

First published in Great Britain in 1996
Reprinted 2003
All rights reserved

John Donne © Sean Haldane 2003

Printed and bound by Q3 Digital/Litho, Loughborough
Tel: 01509 213456
Typesetting and layout by Albion Associates, London
Tel: 020 8852 4646
Cover design by December Publications, Belfast
Tel: 028 90352059

Cover: Detail of a portrait of John Donne by Isaac Oliver, courtesy the National Portrait Gallery, London

Greenwich Exchange Website: www.greenex.co.uk

ISBN 1-871551-23-4

Dedication

To my daughter, Christina Raphaelle, for her help with
'Batter my heart …'

Works by Sean Haldane include:

The Coast and Inland (1968)
Homage to Trumbull Stickney (1968)
The Fright of Time (1970)
The Ocean Everywhere (1970)
What Poetry Is (1970)
Skindiving (1972)
Emotional First Aid (1984)
Desire in Belfast (1992)
Lines from the Stone Age (2000)
Thomas Hardy (2002)

Contents

Chronology

1572   John Donne born at Bread Street, London, some time between 24th January and 19th June.

1576   Donne's father, also John Donne, dies. His mother (née Elizabeth Heywood) remarries Dr John Syminges.

1577 & 1581 Donne's sisters, Elizabeth, Mary and Katherine die.

1584   Donne and his brother Henry matriculate at Hart Hall, Oxford.

1588   John Syminges dies. (Donne's mother remarries Richard Rainsford in 1590). Donne at Cambridge.

1589   Donne in Europe, in Italy, possibly at Battle of Corunna in Spain.

1592   At Lincoln's Inn.

1596   On expedition to Cadiz.

1597   On expedition to the Azores.

1597-8 Begins work as Secretary to Sir Thomas Egerton at York House. Meets Ann More.

1600   Essex confined at York House.

1601   Member of Parliament for Brackley. Essex 'falls': Donne involved in gathering evidence against him. Secret marriage to Ann More (December?).

1602   Imprisoned in Fleet. Released but dismissed by Egerton. Marriage declared valid. Moves to Pyrford.

1603 First child, daughter Constance, born.

1605 Travels with Sir Walter Chute to France.

1606 Moves to Mitcham.

1607 Offered ordination by Bishop of Gloucester, but refuses.

1611 To Belgium and France with Sir Robert Drury.

1612 Still in France, learns of still-born child (his and Ann's eighth). Returns to England. Moves to London, Drury house, with family.

1614 Member of Parliament for Taunton.

1615 Ordained at St Paul's. Becomes Royal Chaplain to James I. Is granted Honorary Doctorate in Divinity at Cambridge.

1617 Ann Donne dies after giving birth to stillborn child. (Seven children survive. Three have died).

1619 Travels to Germany and preaches at Heidelberg.

1621 Installed as Dean of St Paul's.

1623 Ill with relapsing fever.

1630 Becomes finally ill. Makes will.

1631 Donne's mother dies. Donne dies 31st March.

Intoduction

... should she
Be more then woman, shee would get above
All thought of sexe, and thinke to move
My heart to study her, and not to love ...

The *Oxford English Dictionary* cites these lines from Donne's 'The Primrose' as the first use in English of the word 'sex' in the sense we use it now. Previously it had been used only in the biological sense of distinguishing the male and female sexes. Its origin is in Latin and ultimately Indo-European words, meaning 'cut off'. It is related to such words as scissors and secateurs. Not that the Indo-Europeans were proto-Freudians. The implication is not that one sex, woman, has had something cut off, but that 'sex' distinguishes or divides men from women. Modern French retains this sense: the penis or the vagina can each be called 'le sexe' – the place where the division has been made.

Donne's use of 'sex' to mean the activity of coitus lasted well until the mid 20th century. Now, as the century ends, the word is so inclusive it no longer says much either about the difference between men and women or about their consequent uniting in coitus. It has become, paradoxically, asexual and puritan. A *Times* article mentions that a US Senator was observed "having oral sex with another married woman in a parked car." Another article from the USA, about a murder, reports: "he left a party with a male friend, took him to a remote spot, bludgeoned him to death and had sex with his dead body."

Although Donne was an intensely personal poet, his use of the word 'sex' opened up, in a way he could not have foreseen, its use in this impersonal way. People can now talk of 'having sex', as though having a sandwich. Others who might talk, more sentimentally, of 'making love', or 'being together', would not deny that this activity was 'sex', or that it can exist without 'love,' although many people would say that the activity is most intense when sex and love coincide. In Donne's day, the word 'love' did duty not only for the spiritual or emotional but for the sexual activity of loving, as it still does in some dialects of English: for example, in a Canadian bar-room ballad, "the Winnipeg Whore" asks, "How's about a little lovin'? A dollar and a half's the usual fee."

What if Donne had written, "shee would get above/ All thought of love"? He would have made a clear statement about his dilemma: the poem is about a woman who would prefer to have a purely intellectual relationship with him. He goes on to use the word "love" in its physical sense, in worrying that she might persuade him (his heart) to study her rather than make love to her. But in the earlier phrase, "all thought of love" would run into the problem that this high-minded woman might well say something like the immemorial 'Of course I love you – but not in that way'. This is why "shee would get above/ All thought of sexe", which sounds to us so startlingly modern in the context of an Elizabethan poem, is so exactly what Donne has to say.

Although it is possible that the word 'sex' was beginning to be used this way in conversation, it is more likely, given Donne's extreme originality, that he was in fact the first person in English to make a distinction which is so useful that four hundred years later we see it as commonplace. Linguistic innovation seems to occur often where thought is shaped by emotional pressure, as occurs in poetry – and in none more than Donne's. His cast of mind was also influenced by the beginning of the scientific age in which we are now so far embarked. It was probably time for a distinction between spiritual and physical love ('sex') to be made.

By modern standards Donne knew very little about sex. Now, educated people know about ovulation, the function of the menstrual cycle, the generation and microanatomy of the two types of spermatozoa, the fact that hundreds of thousands of them swarm around the comparatively huge ovum, trying to penetrate it until it eventually accepts one then shuts the others out. For Donne, sperm was an "excremental jelly" or "seed". What was in it was anybody's guess. It was only after Donne's death that the Dutchman Leewenhoek examined – "at the expense of his own descendants", it was said in horror at the time – his own sperm under his newly invented microscope, and found it was full of "animalcules". And the existence of the female ovum was unknown until the 19th century. In Donne's time, the prevailing metaphors for sex were biblical and patriarchal: the man sowed his seed (actively) in the woman's (passive) field. However Donne's metaphors, of lovers like burning tapers, or the two halves of a drawing compass, or of their "eyebeams" threaded on "one double string" as love "interanimates two souls" are almost always of a relation between two equals. He writes as much or more of 'we' as of 'I' or 'you'. He even, in his most rebellious early poems and essays, argues that women have every right to be as sexually free as men.

In Donne's time, sex tended to have more dire consequences than for us – at best childbirth, at worst death in childbirth, as well as venereal diseases which no one knew how to protect against, and harsh outcomes if adultery or other transgressions were discovered. But he seems to have been more free than most of his contemporaries to think about it. He already thought in part scientifically, and his poems put some very modern questions, such as: why is it that if one person's genital organs are so physically similar to another's of the same sex, nevertheless we can adore this one and not that?

Even now, the distinction between love and sex is not quite clear. Although we are ready to accept for practical and scientific purposes that sex is not the same as love, there is a longing for them to be, after all, the same. The 20th century has not solved any better than the 16th or 17th the question of why sex and love are sometimes the same, sometimes not. Philosophically, no doubt it is part of the 'mind/ body question'. Scientifically, it is a non issue: loveless sex is cultivated through physical technique. Religiously, it is also a non issue: sexless love is cultivated through spiritual technique, i.e. mysticism.

More than being the first poet in English to distinguish love from sex by the new use of a word, Donne pursued the distinction – and its opposite, the union of the two – as far as any poet ever has. His slightly older contemporary, Shakespeare, also pursued it intensely, but his resolution of it was less successful: love was eventually devoted to the male "Friend" of the Sonnets and the pure daughter figures of his late plays, while sex (though he called it "lust" – not quite the same thing since it can be a one-sided feeling) was turned to the destructive "Dark Lady".

Donne also knew destructive ladies. But eventually he had the luck to fall in love with and marry a woman who was the opposite of destructive. He found "constancy" (an obsession of his) with Ann More, and although he wrote a particularly brutal poem, 'Mummy', about the dark side of "possession" in their marriage, he also wrote some of the most serene poems of sexual/loving happiness in English – only to lose this happiness with the death of Ann after she had given birth to their tenth child (who also died). She had been killed, in effect, by the consequences of their love. Donne seems only to have written one poem in her memory, the despairing 'A Nocturnall upon S. Lucies Day'. But despairing only for himself. Using the word "lust" in a more joyous sense than Shakespeare, and for the moment speaking in the person of Lucy, saint and former goddess of light (therefore an implied 'greater sun'), he addresses:

> You lovers, for whose sake, the lesser Sunne
>   At this time to the Goat is runne
>   To fetch new lust, and give it you,
>   Enjoy your summer all ...

Modern readers, and lovers, still come to Donne, and although the effect of his poems can be shatteringly sad at times – he knew, as does any honest person, as much failure as success in love – his experience is so close to the bone that it may help us to some measure of truth, and enable us better to 'enjoy our summer', even as, like Donne as the same poem ends, we are left on the shortest day of the year (which under the old calendar coincided with St Lucy's day) to keep:

> This houre her Vigill, and her Eve, since this
> Both the yeares, and the dayes deep midnight is.

1   Life

"John Donne, Ann Donne, Undone." This famous gloss which, according to Walton, Donne wrote in the margin of a letter in 1601, after his secret marriage to Ann More had been revealed, summarises the pivotal moment around which his life seems to hinge. Until then his worldly advance had been steady, after then it turned to decline, reversed only when he was ordained, just before Ann's death.

The pun on Donne and "done" was always obvious (both words were pronounced the same, although to rhyme with 'shone'), and Donne used it in one of his poems, the 'Hymn to God the Father'. (This, and the brilliance of the gloss, are reasons for assuming that the unreliable and anecdotal Walton was accurate for once, and that Donne did in fact write it. His more fussy but less sensible modern biographer R.C. Bald, who is ready to take Walton seriously in dubious accounts of Donne's pious asseverations on his deathbed, chooses to discount the gloss and assumes that someone unknown concocted it). Donne is saying first that John is 'done', in the sense of 'done for', and perhaps in the sense of 'done with' or 'finished': later he would refer to his earlier self as "Jack Donne". Now he was no longer a Jack, in the sense of Shakespeare's sonnet 128 where a jack is a penis or a knave (as in the card pack): he would have to be grown up – John. Secondly, Ann is 'done', in the sense, lively to the Elizabethans, of having been sexually had. And thirdly, not only is he himself "undone" (destroyed) but he is no longer the same Donne as before. He is also probably taking some innocent pleasure in writing Ann's new married name and linking it with his own in the marriage tie – which, he may have worried since an attempt was being made to disallow it, might in fact be undone. And even if it was not, what would the catastrophic reactions to his marriage do to his relationship with Ann?

Donne may not have known Skelton's "Mistress Anne/ I am your man." But he was now Ann's man, and was to remain so even after her death, in spite of his willed devotion to Christianity:

> Since she whom I lov'd hath payd her last debt
> To Nature and to hers, and my good is dead,

And her Soule early into heaven ravished,
Wholly on heavenly things my mind is sett.

The bare bones of Donne's life – dates and major known events –
are catalogued in the Chronology. But he would have been
uninterested in these bare bones: the "bracelet of bright hair about
the bone" was what he lived for – his relation with others, especially
women, and his friends. To take 1601 as an example, the year of
"John Donne, Ann Donne, Undone", it was Donne's personal crisis
that affected his being and his poetry, not his active involvement in
the public drama of the Essex rebellion. He knew Essex, could sum
up his character astutely in a letter, and probably helped draw up the
legal case against him, but this had no discernible effect on his poetry
or, it can be assumed, his inner life.

What follows here is a brief account of what seem to have been
the key events in Donne's life, those which appear twice, as it were:
in his biography and in his poems.

Donne was probably born in the first half of 1572, in London.
His father was a prosperous member of the Ironmongers' Company,
and connected with a Welsh family called Dwn. (The word means
'brown' in the Celtic languages, as does 'dun' in English). His mother
was a daughter of John Heywood, a Coventry man who wrote plays
and songs for the Court and for other performances in the early years
of Elizabeth I's reign. In spite of the Reformation, the Heywoods
remained Catholic. Donne's uncle, Jasper Heywood, was a famous
Jesuit who could only enter England from the Continent secretly (he
had been exiled after a period of imprisonment in the Tower of
London), and as Donne later put it, "I had my first breeding and
conversation with men of suppressed and afflicted religion,
accustomed to the despite of death and hungry of an imagined
martyrdom." (This environment and the implications of 'recusancy',
conflicts of loyalty between church and monarch, and the horror of
becoming an 'apostate' as Donne eventually did, are thoroughly
explored in John Carey's study, *John Donne. Life, Mind and Art*.)

The intensity of this half-persecuted Catholicism may have been
exacerbated by the fact that Donne was just under four years old
when his Anglican father died, and his relationship with his mother
seems to have been very close. He had a younger brother, Henry, and
two older and two younger sisters – although three of these sisters

2

died young. Some of his character, and his later capacity for friendship, as well as love, with women may originate in this childhood among women. However, his mother married again when he was aged only five, to a middle-aged and very distinguished medical doctor. (When her second husband died, she married a third time). It is fruitless to speculate about the effects of heredity on Donne: the Welsh streak was some generations back, and although it is sometimes stated that on his mother's side he was descended from the famous Sir Thomas More, this is not so – the connection was by marriage. The most that can be said is that on his mother's side his immediate ancestors seem to have been of exceptional ability, and this can also be assumed for his very successful father. It is odd how many poets and musicians are descended, respectively, from minor versifiers or instrumentalists. But the odds have not been properly worked out. If poets are born not made, as seems likely, Donne's maternal grandfather's having written songs and plays may reflect a family talent with words and music. But none of us, so far, can be convincingly explained away with reference either to our heredity or to the usually self-fulfilling analysis of environment by psychologists of various schools.

Of more immediate interest are the expectations Donne may have felt from his parents, either through what they said or from his childhood observation of them. As often happens, eventually he seems to have fulfilled the expectations of both parents – but in an unexpected way. His mother may have wanted him to be a Jesuit priest: instead he became an Anglican one. His father may have wanted him to be a success in the world: instead he was a success in the church. It is safe to say that neither would have wanted him to be a poet.

It was only after Donne that Henry Vaughan became the first poet in English to write about his childhood: "Happy those early days when I/ Shin'd in my Angel-infancy!" Elizabethan children in paintings are like little adults. Donne was sent to Oxford when he was aged 12. Although he later wrote affectionately in a letter about his own "gamesome" children by the fireside, the gamesomeness of Elizabethan children swiftly became of an adult sort (drinking, rowdying, etc.), and study was arduous. Donne seems to have been something of a swot, and his habit of taking extensive notes on any book he read was noticed already at Oxford. (By the end of his life he had, according to Walton, "the resultance of 1400 Authors, most of them abridged and analysed with his own hand".) He was enrolled at Hart Hall (where Hertford College is now), but because of his Catholicism did not take a degree (at which he would have had to swear to the Anglican 39 Articles) and after three years was sent to Cambridge for another three. (Cambridge being less efficient than Oxford, at that time at least, there is no record of which college he went to). At university he met many of his lifelong friends, including two recipients of later verse letters, Goodyer and Wotton.

After Cambridge, in 1589, he seems to have gone on a European tour. The details are obscure, in Bald's view, because he may have travelled not only in Italy, to Venice, but to Spain, which was against the law for Englishmen. It is assumed he may have met Jasper Heywood and other English Catholic exiles. Although there are some references in his sermons to scenes which may be European, there are none in his poems – except perhaps for *Elegy* XVI, in which he rejects an offer by his beloved (almost certainly Ann More) to accompany him in secret on a journey, disguised as a page-boy, with the argument that "Th'indifferent [sexually ambivert] Italian, as we passe/ His warme land, well content to think thee Page,/ Will hunt thee with such lust ..." (This has outraged progressive 20th century critics). He does seem to have read widely in Italian and Spanish, and he could write a good letter in French (as well as knowing Latin, of course, and later in life, Greek and Hebrew), but it is impossible to distinguish, in his knowledge, what was learnt at first hand and what from books.

A theory discussed by Donne's biographers (see Bald and Parker) is that his visit to Spain may have preceded his tour of the rest of Europe, and that he was part of a military expedition (with many gentleman volunteers) under Francis Drake and John Norreys which besieged Corunna in 1589. This would explain his epigram 'Fall of a Wall', which describes a known incident:

> Under an undermin'd and shot-bruised wall
> A too-bold Captaine perish'd by the fall,
> Whose brave misfortune, happiest men envi'd,
> That had a towne for tombe, his bones to hide.

Military service would also explain the fact that he clutches a sword in the first known portrait of him, in 1591, thought to be a copy of a lost original by Nicholas Hilliard (for whose brilliant miniatures, see the collection in the National Portrait Gallery in London). The inscription on the portrait gives his age as 18. He has lank hair, large but direct-looking eyes widely spaced, high cheekbones, a neat moustache, and long, irregularly shaped nose.

In 1592, he began the study of law at Lincoln's Inn. Until 1615, when he was ordained, law provided him with his bread and butter – or at least whatever of it was not received in the form of his own and his wife's family money, and gifts and unreturned loans from patrons. His activities as private secretary to, in effect, what we would call a Minister, as researcher for friends involved in litigation, and even as a member of parliament, all depended on his expertise in law. He despised the law, and lawyers – see *Satire* II. But he was always something of a wrangler. His poems are full of arguments. And the transition, eventually, to the church was not inconsistent with the law. After all, there is God's law.

At Lincoln's Inn, Donne was Master of the Revels, with the duty of organising entertainment, plays, and dinners. But these were plague years, and his studies were often interrupted. He was also known as "a great visitor of Ladies." One of these, according to a manuscript (not in Donne's hand) of 'Confined Love' must have been "Mrs P". This early poem, among the cluster which celebrates change and inconstancy ("Why should I/ Abjure my so much lov'd variety?"), like the *Paradoxes* he was writing in prose, is annotated, ironically no doubt: "To the wor: [i.e. worthiest] of all my Lou [loves] my virtuous Mrs P. A Song."

Who was Mrs P? The only 'Ps' who figure in Donne's life at about this time are the brothers Edward and Henry Parvish. Donne presented a copy of a German book on Cosmography to Edward, who seems to have worked with his brother, according to Bald, "the business magnate who among his other activities, ran a forwarding service for mail, money and goods, of which Henry Wotton [Donne's friend] availed himself for his first visit to Europe in 1589" – the year Donne is conjectured to have travelled there. No one has paid any attention to "Mrs P". It is tempting to speculate that she might be Mrs Parvish, and also the married woman who figures in, *Elegies* I and XII, who slips off to fornicate with Donne while her (business magnate?) husband, "swolne, and pamper'd with great fare,/ Sits down, and snorts, cag'd in his basket chaire"

Donne seems to have been living independently on a legacy of £750 from his father, but family reality became more grim in 1593, when his brother Henry died from the plague while confined in Newgate because of involvement in a supposed Catholic plot. It is thought that, although Donne's usual voracious reading was concentrated at the time in Catholic theology, his only brother's death caused him to become bitter against the Catholic church. More likely, it caused him to reject narrowness: he later stated that all the churches – Calvinism, Anglicanism, Catholicism – were different beams of the same light. And *Satire* III, written at about this time, can be read as against the hypocrites of any branch of Christianity.

During his Lincoln's Inn years, Donne may also have visited friends at Oxford, and it is conjectured that he might have met, either there or in London, Magdalen Herbert, the mother of his young friend Edward Herbert. Donne and she were to remain friends, on and off, until he officiated at her funeral in 1627. She was an intellectual, and devout, but obviously not without zest: when a widow and above the age of 40, she married Sir John Danvers who was half her age. In the 1590s she lived at Montgomery Castle, on the Welsh border, and 'The Primrose' and 'The Blossom' have been associated with her. (In early April, this "primrose hill" is still covered with primroses, and blossom is out on bare fruit tree branches.) It is fairly clear from the poems that Donne wanted Magdalen Herbert to think of 'sex' but she preferred to think of ideas: he hied himself back to London "There, to another friend, whom wee shall finde/ As glad to have my body, as my minde."

The Lothian portrait of Donne in 1595 presents him in a fashionable melancholy pose. He is dressed in black but with an elaborate lace collar. This is the same face as in 1591, with the big nose and eyes, but the lips are more sensual, the expression more confident: nowadays he would make a suitable rock star.

In 1596 and 1597 Donne was a gentleman volunteer on two military expeditions, one to Cadiz, one to the Azores. Some of the *Epigrams* and his verse letters 'The Calme' and 'The Storme' describe his experiences. The expeditions were led by Essex and by Ralegh, whom Donne does not seem to have known then (he would have been an exalted figure at the time, though soon due to fall) although he wrote a conventional 'Come live with me' poem, based on Catullus, which seems to compete with Ralegh's version and with Marlowe's. He may have met Marlowe, through Cambridge connections, and his Elegies seem to take off from Marlowe's versions of those in Ovid's *Amores*. (He is thought to have met Ralegh only later, in the early 1600s, when Ralegh was imprisoned by James I in the Tower of London along with the 'Wizard' Earl of Northumberland, a close friend of Donne's, and Donne probably visited both men for conversations about scientific discoveries). He certainly knew Jonson, and possibly Shakespeare, and he frequented the Mitre and Mermaid taverns as they did.

Donne was not wounded in his military expeditions, and he may have been mainly a spectator. He discovered, at least, that he was – Catholic or not – deeply loyal to "England to whom we'owe, what we be, and have." The expeditions had no effect on his more deeply felt poems. The experience of war would not necessarily have even produced the kind of reflections on death that we have become used to since the First World War poets, since the Elizabethans were a less pampered lot before they experienced war: death in its various ugly forms was commonplace in Donne's family and all around him. However, he witnessed a sight at Cadiz which even the battle-hardened Ralegh found terrible, the foundering and explosion of the Spanish ship, the *San Felipe*. Donne described this in an epigram which ends:

So all were lost, which in the ship were found,
They in the sea being burnt, they in the burnt ship drown'd.

In 1597 Donne gained a position as one of the secretaries (not the chief one, as is sometimes said) of Sir Thomas Egerton, Lord Keeper of the Seal, an immensely powerful post for which there is no equivalent (thank God) today. Donne performed legal work for Egerton, was briefly a member of parliament (a matter of being nominated and accepted without popular vote, in a constituency, Brackley in Northamptonshire, which he had probably never seen), and lived with Egerton and his family at York House, between the Strand and the river. It was here that he lived through part of the Essex drama in 1600.

Possibly he felt exuberant enough to want to publish his poems, but then thought better of it. In January 1600, what might have been one of the most extraordinary books in the history of English poetry was registered for publication but did not appear: 'Amours by J.D. with certen other sonnetes by W.S.'

Most important, though, was his meeting in 1597 with the 14 year old Ann More, Egerton's second wife's niece. They rapidly became lovers or almost lovers. Ann seems to have shuttled between York House and the country where her father lived (her mother was dead), so there were long separations. This is the background of some of the *Elegies*, and some of the *Songs and Sonets*. Ann was, in many of these poems, his "Angel" – pronounced then "Anngel".

"Per Rachel ho servito non per Lea". It is not known when Donne began inscribing this Petrarchan tag in his books. The reference is to Genesis XXIX, where Jacob marries the virtuous Rachel after serving her for seven years as required by her father Laban, but has first slept with her sister Leah who, with Rachel's knowledge, has pretended to be Rachel. Jacob has already sired sons on Leah and on her maid, and on Rachel's maid, before Rachel, thought to be barren, conceives Joseph after eating grated mandrake root. (Donne refers frequently in his poems to the legend of the mandrake, the man-shaped plant which shrieks when dug up). It seems likely that Donne began using the motto after falling in love with Ann. Its message is, in effect, 'Even though I have gone to bed with and served sexually a number of women, the woman I have truly served is the pure mother of my legitimate children.'

At the end of 1601, Donne and Ann were secretly married. Her father could not be won over, in spite of the efforts of the eccentric 'Wizard Earl' acting on Donne's behalf as a go-between, and he worked on Egerton to sack Donne. Donne spent some weeks in prison, but it was the loss of his job which proved fatal, as he knew it would, to his reputation. "John Donne, Ann Donne, Undone."

Eventually, however, the marriage was recognised by the Court of High Commission as valid, and Donne and Ann were able to live together, at Pyrford in Surrey, supported at first by Donne's friend Francis Wolley, for whom Donne did legal work, then eventually, as Ann's father relented, by his settlement on her of £80 per year. Ann bore children at the rate of about one a year. The first, a daughter, was called – in a tribute, probably, both to Donne's own discovery of lasting love, and to Ann's devotion to him through difficult events – Constance.

In 1605 Donne travelled to France in the company of a friend, Sir Walter Chute. He was desperate to gain advancement, perhaps in diplomatic work. On his return he and his family moved to Mitcham, from which he could travel easily to London, where he had a rented room on the Strand. He seems to have done miscellaneous legal work. He probably discussed science with the Wizard Earl and with Ralegh to whom he was now related by marriage. (Lady Ralegh's brother Sir Nicholas Carey had married one of Ann's sisters). He read in theology. He wrote *Biathanatos,* his study of suicide, and suffered from depression and ill health. The most terrible of his poems to Ann, 'Mummy', describes his state.

He seems to have tried to redeem his despair, and his sense of the physical consequences of love – in the form of children, ill health and exhaustion for Ann, ill health (rheumatic and stomach troubles) and debts for him – by concocting a more or less ideal love for two patronesses: Lucy, Countess of Bedford (whom he had met at York House when she was a girl) and the Countess of Huntingdon. There are some rather sordid letters to friends in which he discusses such hopes as that the Countess of Bedford would pay off his debts. (She offered to do so but only sent £30, which caused him to rage). She was known as brilliant, wrote verses, and was a sort of public Muse: Ben Jonson also wrote poems to her. She was godmother to one of Donne's daughters – Lucy. (There is no record of how Ann took all this). But no matter how hard he tried, Donne's verses to these patronesses are, apart from the occasional line of poetry, merely verses. He may have had a genuine crush on a young woman called Bridget White of whom we know nothing except that she did not return his interest. There is no suggestion from any source that he was ever unfaithful to Ann. But, tellingly, he named a daughter Bridget. (Or had he discovered in his studies the ancient British sun goddess Brigit, like St Lucy, the source of light?)

Donne wrote many letters to his friends during these years (he had a pact to write to the amiable Henry Goodyer every week), but as was the form then, they are more like discursive essays, and it was not done to mention family matters. Occasionally, however, these break through. He describes the house at Mitcham as his "hospital" or his "prison". In 1607 he wrote to Goodyer as Ann was giving birth to a son, Francis, upstairs: "her anguish, and my fears, and hopes ... all narrowed themselves, and met in Via Regia, which is the consideration of our selves, and God ..." "Via Regia", the royal way, is loaded here with meaning on several levels, suggesting his concern with his and Ann's and his family's worldly 'selves' at the same time as with God and religion. Via Regia means Christ's Way into Bethlehem. It means 'the right way', i.e. the Christian one. It also means the right way in alchemy to arrive at the manufacture of gold. And it means the vagina: Ann's, through which her anguish and his fears and hopes literally narrowed themselves to emerge as a new son – of God, like Christ.

If Donne had a difficulty with Ann, about which he must have felt guilty, especially when he wrote verses to intellectual ladies, it was that she was not herself intellectual. It can be assumed that she was highly intelligent – otherwise Donne would not have devoted himself to her. (Modern psychological studies suggest that the quality in which spouses are most likely to be equally matched is intelligence). But she had never had the chance to be educated, and with her many children, to whom she was devoted, she would not have spent time reading. As Donne sat with her by the fireside at Mitcham with his "gamesome children", his head must often have been churning. And at this time, poetry and religious studies were not mutually exclusive. Part of his turning back to religion, which he had in effect abandoned, seems to have been the tormenting guilt he felt about having got Ann into this mess, a "wretched fortune". He wrote most of his religious poems at this time, as well as poems to Ann. Prison or not, Mitcham was better for his poetry than London turned out to be when he moved there in 1612. The impetus for this move may have come from the previous year, when on another long journey to France (there seem to have been financial advantages to these journeys) he saw an 'apparition' of Ann walking with a dead child in her arms, and later learned by letter that she had had a stillborn baby.

He had been cultivating some of the various disgusting (there is no other word for them) courtiers who surrounded the equally disgusting James I. James took an interest in Donne – seemingly to encourage him in his worldly ambitions, but in the end to persuade him into holy orders. It is difficult to comprehend how Donne, at least an acquaintance of Ralegh, and undoubtedly aware that Ralegh was a true poet in spite of his worldly faults, could have described this monster king (who had imprisoned Ralegh and would have him executed in 1618) in a sermon as "great and good". There is no point in telling in detail the story of Donne's attempts to gain advancement, especially once the desperate but at least imaginative gambles of seeking employment in Ireland and in the colony of Virginia had failed. As Bald summarizes his gloomy account:

> he appears as one who had mastered at last the arts of the courtier, and it is clear, even when he finally turned to the Church, that he did not intend to abandon those arts, but to rise by them. At no period of his life does he appear less unselfish, more self-seeking. The truth seems to be that these qualities in him were not essential and permanent traits of his character, rather they were symptoms of his despair – not the despair of one who feels that he has been denied salvation, but that of one whom success eludes in spite of all his efforts.

He was ordained in January 1614/1615, became chaplain to the King, and soon afterward was granted a Doctorate in Divinity at Cambridge. He had been thinking once again of publishing his poems, but not, apparently in the same spirit as in 1600, when publication would have been for the poetry's sake. Now publication, as it appears from letters he wrote to friends asking them to send him copies of poems of his they had been keeping, would have been a way of putting poetry behind him and almost certainly of suppressing whatever was not respectable. He would presumably have published those of his divine poems which had already been written, and such set pieces as the 'Anniversaries', the first of which had been already published in 1611, and the second of which would appear along with the first again, in 1621. Ben Jonson, in his conversations with Drummond of Hawthornden in 1618, said that Donne "since he was made Doctor repenteth highlie and seeketh to destroy all his poems."

A portrait painted in 1616 shows a new dapper Dr Donne, with trimmed beard and prim mouth. But there are bags under sad-looking eyes. As usual he is in black: the black of the melancholy poet become the proper black of the priest.

On the 15th August, Assumption Day, 1617, Ann Donne died, of exhaustion after giving birth to a still-born child. She was aged 33. Donne soon erected a monument to her, now destroyed, at St Clement Danes, which described her, in Latin, as the chosen of women, the most delightful, the dearest of wives, the most chaste, the most pious and the most indulgent of mothers, and stated that her husband, the most miserable of men, was the beloved of her as she was the beloved of him. This may, understandably, be a simplification. There is some indication from the poems that Ann was not so docile as she is often assumed to have been.

Donne went almost mad, and his friends wondered if he would live. Eventually foreign travel, the Deanship of St Paul's, and the support of friends brought him out of it.

Bald writes about Donne's "deepened sense of Christian truth", and quotes a commentator (one G.R. Potter) on how he "became more perceptive" about "the glory of God's love to man", and "awakened to an emotional as well as an intellectual conviction that Christ has redeemed mankind", and that "both of these developments appear first in sermons preached shortly after the death of his wife."

But, no matter how one feels about Christianity, such mealy-mouthed clichés are surely not much consolation for the diminution of Donne's poetic flame, left to flicker occasionally in the admittedly wonderful prose of his sermons – many of whose images are rehashes from poems. He did write a few more divine poems, and not least, he probably wrote his last pagan (in the sense of non-Christian) poem, the 'Nocturnal upon S. Lucies day', in which the darkly invisible figure of Lucy ('Light') is less that of a saint than of a Goddess of the turning year.

His life became conventional, as probably it had to be if he was to care for his children (to whom he had promised he would not remarry), although it seems too much when he marries the dutiful Constance off to a superannuated but rich actor, Sir Edward Alleyn, who was in his sixties. (Constance did all right in the end: when Alleyn died and left her his money, she married a younger man). To give him credit, there are signs Donne fretted about this: he argued about money with Alleyn, who reproached him for using language more fitted to his younger days.

The story of Donne's preparation for death in 1631, wrapping himself for practice in his own shroud, is well known. In his monument in St Paul's, which survived the Fire of 1666, the face based on his death mask has been described as serene but seems to portray a Velasquez-like, elongated resignation.

The moment of "John Donne, Ann Donne, Undone" was one in which Donne's outer life (his history) and his inner one (his poetry) came together. But such moments are infrequent in the life of a poet. Much of anyone's life is, after all, merely banal – 'history'. (Death actually, as when the killer draws his gun and says: "You're history.") History includes much of anyone's thinking. Poetry, however, is new thought – otherwise it would not compel the poet, its victim as it were, to write it. As the 20th century American poet Laura Riding said, poetry, like humour, is "an interruption in the life of habit." The clichés and routine considerations that normally fill the mind are suddenly displaced by a rush of clear thought, accompanied by emotion and autonomic sensations (A.E. Housman provided an almost clinical description of these: watering eyes, tightening of the throat, "frissons"), in which language seems to appear already organised into whatever rhythms, verbal music and forms the poet has absorbed from his or her tradition. What the poem has to say is a surprise to the poet, and it may be inconsistent with his or her ordinary prose beliefs. There are two stories or histories in a poet's life: the story of his or her life as a human being, which includes the writing of the poems themselves; and the story told in the poems.

The first story, in Donne's case, is meticulously told in R.C. Bald's standard biography, to which only occasionally a newly discovered fact can be added. This necessary history is (to use an irresistible pun) so baldly factual that it succeeds in making Donne's life dull. (By far a more readable and enjoyable biography, although it is less detailed, is the illustrated one by Derek Parker). The level of Bald's appreciation of Donne can be deduced from his banal comment that Donne is "one of the really significant figures in the history of English literature." Unless a poem is blatantly part of public history (as in Donne's epigram about the battle of Cadiz), Bald does not allow it to enter into Donne's personal story. He suffers from the academic fallacy that poetry is a form of prose translated into verse, rather than a unique kind of thought and utterance. (The late 19th century American poet Trumbull Stickney, writing in French, called it "la pensée musicale"). Bald refers to Donne's "poetic heightening to a situation", to poems in which "fiction outweighs the fact", and to other critics' "misinterpretations" of poems by taking them literally. His excuse for this attitude is that it has "been very effectively put by W.H. Auden: 'What makes it difficult for a poet not to tell lies is that, in poetry, all facts and all beliefs cease to be true or false and become interesting possibilities.'" But Auden had two reasons for wanting poetry to be evasive – as indeed his own verse succeeds in being: that he did not want to 'come out' as a homosexual in his verse (although he did so cheerfully enough in life), and that when his original élan rapidly faded he took to "synthesising" his works using quotations from his contemporaries. In time he may be seen more as a versifier than a poet, but no matter how his work is estimated, it is much different from Donne's which, as most readers' intuition will tell them, is emotionally intense and therefore likely to be real. Bald undoes his case that Donne's poems are largely fictional by remarking that "one can see how such a poem as the elegy 'The Perfume' would have started rumours that it would be difficult to kill."

Donne's poems caused him problems. They embarrassed him. This is why he tried to suppress them in later life, and remarked in a letter to an acquaintance to whom he was sending a new religious poem, "I did best when I had least truth for my subjects." But even in earlier life he was forbidden by Elizabethan etiquette (which would be worth a revival in our world of 15 minute fame) from taking pride in his poems. He wrote to a friend about his first acquaintance with the Countess of Huntingdon:

> that knowledge which she hath of me, was in the beginning of a graver course, then [than] of a Poet, into which (that I may also keep my dignity) I would not seem to relapse. The Spanish proverb informes me, that he is a fool which cannot make one Sonnet, and he is mad which makes two.

Bald quotes in support of his incuriosity about the literal in Donne's poems the famous:

> Who ever guesses, thinks or dreams he knowes who is my mistris, wither by this curse ...

and concludes: "in all these poems the states and attitudes of mind revealed are more significant than the name of any woman." (Significant of what?) If Donne was having a secret affair with a married woman, as some of the *Elegies* zestfully describe (unless they are to be seen as academic exercises or the 'heightening' in verse of a prose fiction), he might well feel incensed at having her

14

name revealed. But in fact the poem is about something more than hiding a woman's name (he does not even mention the word 'name'), it is about hiding her identity. Identity, as we shall see in analysing various of the love poems, obsessed Donne. Reading the lines for what they say at their first literal level, Donne is incensed by the possibility that a reader of his poems will through them know "who is" his mistress, as intimately as he, her lover, knows who she is – and has been telling in poetry. It is a poem about his jealousy of his possible readers. After all – and he must have felt the paradox (he thought easily in paradoxes) – what gives his poems their life is the uniqueness, 'who she is', of his mistress. He has even revealed the uniqueness, for him, of her "best loved part" in his poems, and he is angry at himself and at his readers whom he tries to scare off from coming too close.

It is 'who she is', in her best loved part and in all the rest of her self and her actions (Donne's poems are full of descriptions of his woman loves through their actions), that inspires his poems. Far from a woman's name, or more profoundly, her identity, being less "significant" than "states and attitudes of mind", these states and attitudes depend, in the poems, entirely on her. A great poem does not exist without a great Muse. Or, phrased differently, the 'Thou' or 'Other' to whom any poem (whether by a woman or a man) is written is as important in the poem's genesis as the writer.

Donne's critical editors (even Grierson, and especially Helen Gardner and John Carey) inevitably assume that he wrote poems deliberately, as an artistic effort. But this does not correspond to the experience of poets. All readers will have experienced moments of sudden 'inspiration' in which words or actions come unerringly and feel 'right'. Poems, for some people whom the world eventually calls poets, (although except when they are writing poems they may not very often feel like anything other than ordinary human beings), come at such moments. It is important to realise this when considering the life and work of Donne. He must no doubt have applied considerable thought and skill to his poems, but as Robert Frost put it, "a poem can be worked over once it is in being, but it can't be worked into being". The poems first worked on Donne, not the other way around.

Another complication is that although, as Robert Graves has said, a person's poetry may be a "spiritual autobiography", the events of this autobiography are not all written down in chronological order.

15

Although some of Donne's poems have the air of immediacy – of being written excitedly on the morning after the night before, or of taking off from lines which may have formed in his mind even during the events they describe – they may in fact have been written in a sudden vivid recall of events many years later. As Graves said in conversation when aged 66, "Sometimes I find myself writing poems I should have written 40 years ago."

Two modern critics, Carey and Redpath, have, in contrast to the Bald approach of separating life from poetry, taken some pains with the chronology of Donne's poems. Carey's Oxford edition of 1990 claims to be a new arrangement of the poems in chronological order, but in fact there are few changes from the order of the 1635 edition (the first, after the original 1633 edition, to group the poems as we now see them, into *Elegies, Satires, Songs and Sonets* etc.) which is usually followed. The *Satires* are interspersed with the *Elegies*, which is not new, and these two genres are seen as the product of the 1590s. The *Songs and Sonets* are as usual printed as a separate group, but with the comment that they were all written after 1603. It is a tidy idea that for the first 15 years or so of his poetic life Donne wrote only in the iambic couplets we see in the *Elegies, Satires,* and verse letters – with the occasional fashionable *Epigram* thrown in – and that he then entered a new phase where he only wrote in the multiplicity of lyrical forms we see in the *Songs and Sonets*. This progress by formal stages may represent the way professors think. But it is not the way poets write. It is likely that Donne's forms varied with what he had to say, and that the earlier of the *Songs and Sonets* were written in the 1590s, the period of the *Elegies* and the *Satires* – as in fact recognised by most editors, from Grierson onwards.

Since so much of Donne's history is known, it is impossible to read his poems naively. But it is worth the exercise to put aside preconceptions, and the explicit data of the verse letters to friends, and to try and discern from internal evidence alone whatever story emerges from the *Elegies* and the *Songs and Sonets*.

There is no story in the sense of an obvious sequence, such as can be derived from sonnet sequences from Petrarch through to Shakespeare. Donne would have probably disdained such a scheme.

It has been suggested, even, that his use of the word *Sonets* in his title (assuming he had anything to do with the title of either the collection or the individual poems, which could have been added by transcribers and editors) was deliberately defiant. The only formal 14 line sonnet among his love poems is the rather slight 'The Token', and the poems represent a great variety of forms and situations: although most tell a self-contained story in a passionate narrative, there is no linking narrative in the prose sense. (So many traditional sonnet sequences are dud as poetry because the concept of a sequence requires a plan, and is in effect a prose project.) As mentioned, Donne inscribed a motto taken from Petrarch on the flyleaf of most of the books in his library: "Per Rachel ho servito non per Lea". Redpath traces many Petrarchan and anti-Petrarchan allusions in Donne's poetry. But, as a proverb has it, "to a hammer, everything is a nail", and Redpath's nail is Petrarch. Since where Donne has taken an image or an idea from his reading it is always transformed radically to his poem's ends, the academic game of mix-and-match is usually a distraction from what is most important about the poem – what it says.

Donne seems to have been under some pressure from political patrons to put together a collection in 1615, and there has been some speculation that the manuscript of this, (though the collection did not appear), forms the base of the 1633 and 1635 editions. Neither edition presents a sequence. But it becomes evident that, especially in the 1635 edition which is most commonly followed, some of the poems are clustered according to theme or tone. Other poems seem anomalous or out of place.

Since the *Elegies* and the *Songs and Sonets* are almost all love poems, it seems reasonable to look for their story in terms of whom they seem to have been written to or about. They can be clustered into groups as follows:

1) Poems about inconstancy and change, rather along the lines of Donne's prose *Paradoxes,* known to have been written in the 1590s. They might, in a sense, have been written to anyone, and they celebrate promiscuity.

2) Poems about 'mistresses' with whom he had secret and perhaps long-lasting affairs, although still characterised by inconstancy and change. There seem to have been two of these, one with

protective parents, another with a jealous husband. Both relationships seem to have ended with 'betrayal' by the mistress.

3) Poems about the early stages of a love affair with a young
   girl, which is taken very seriously and causes a change of the
   poet's view, towards constancy.
4) Poems about a constant domestic relationship or marriage, in
   which questions of possession, partings, faithfulness, devotion
   and support in sadness predominate.
5) Poems about an intellectual, possibly Platonic, but frustrating
   relationship with a woman who holds a position of power.

Returning to what is known of Donne's life, it seems reasonable to
suppose that the poems of inconstancy, as it were, (1 & 2 above)
were written before he met Ann More, and that the poems of
constancy (3 & 4 above) are about their early love and subsequent
marriage. The 'Platonic' poems (5 above) were most probably written
to Magdalen Herbert. There is a wide range of experience in Donne's
relationships – not in the crude statistical sense that he had relationships with this or that many women, but in the sense that these
relationships vary so much in their nature, although Donne
characteristically seems to have believed passionately in each
relationship on its own terms. Perhaps as a consequence of that intense
Catholic upbringing by a beloved mother who always 'kept the faith',
Donne always seems to have struggled to stay faithful to his idea of
what his relationship was – even if it was one of inconstancy. Although
the Lothian portrait shows him as a self-conscious rebel, he was
never a rebel without a cause. And he had the intellect and training
to argue or to wrangle for any cause. Yet his passionate intensity
(that quality so oddly denigrated by Yeats: it is the best, not the cold
and calculating worst, who are "full of passionate intensity") meant
he could never deny the truth of his senses. Hence the struggle, the
paradoxes, his emotional rebellion first against inconstancy, then
against constancy, even as he argued for them – which makes poetry.
Only when in later life he was licensed by the church to preach (rather
than by his mistress to let his roving hands go ...), did his arguments
become consistent – which makes prose.

2   Poems of Inconstancy

Donne always seems to have been 'flash'– no shrinking violet. Even the more retiring of the two early portraits shows his hand on a sword. For all we know, he composed lost religious homilies or sentimental ditties in adolescence, but his first public appearance was as the conspicuously clever student at Lincoln's Inn, Master of Revels (in a plague year!), a "visitor of ladies", and author of widely circulated *Satires* and love poems – probably some of the *Songs and Sonets* and some of the *Elegies*.

One of the earliest of Donne's poems may be the 'Epithalamion made at Lincoln's Inne' which contains a passage about how the bride:

> ... at the Bridegroome's wish'd approach doth lye,
> Like an appointed lambe, when tenderly
> The priest comes on his knees t'embowell her ...

Since Lincoln's Inn was not known for its marriages (it was an all male scholastic barracks), and Donne was Master of the Revels, it is almost certain that the 'Epithalamion' was a spoof on the one just published by Edmond Spenser (and 'acclaimed', as our modern newspapers would say). One can imagine a half-drunken student shuffling priest-like on his knees toward another male student dressed in drag lying like a lamb on an altar, as the lines are declaimed. (This sort of horseplay is common in Jonson's plays). However, since Donne took these things seriously, at bottom, his spoof hovers on the edge of being a serious poem, and this has caused some critical confusion. In particular, it has been misinterpreted by John Carey who in turn is misinterpreted by an avowedly feminist critic, Stevie Davies. Davies runs rampant with the horrors of the "aroused" Carey's supposed fantasy (and Donne's) of "ripping out guts through the tender sexual parts."

But Donne wrote "embowel". He did not write 'disembowel'. However, Carey states that "'Embowell' means the same as 'disembowel', the dictionary tells us." It doesn't. The Oxford dictionaries give two meanings of 'embowell', with dates and examples. The first meaning, from 1521, is indeed 'disembowel', abbreviated. But the second meaning, from 1596, is: "put or convey into the bowels or depths". The 1596 example of this usage is from a biography of Francis Drake, where winds are described as being "embowelled" in a bladder. Then there is an example from a sermon given in 1629 – by Donne himself: "All was embowelled and enwombed in the waters."

What Donne means by "t'embowell her" is 'to fill her bowel'. By which he means her vagina, which was anatomically considered a bowel (or gut) in those days. He is probably also referring to the man's penis, anatomically considered to be an extension of bowel, as if to say 'to empenis' her – as the man is, in a sense, giving her his penis, as part of his "wish'd approach". There is some evidence that the use of lamb's gut as a condom was beginning to be current in the 1590s: although Donne is hardly writing about this, the idea of lamb's gut or bowel as having a texture like that of the penis and vagina may be present. And finally, he is saying something quite subtle about the sexual experience of the girl becoming a woman (which, politically correct or not in today's terms, was considered to occur when a virgin first experienced coitus: as emphasised in the epithalamion's refrain, "Tonight put on perfection, and a woman's name" – in itself a new twist by Donne, since normally virginity, not womanhood, was considered to be perfection). He is saying that the man is 'giving her a bowel', that is by entering the vagina which has never been entered before, he is giving to her the possibility of feeling what has not been felt before. He is, in the old-fashioned phrase, 'awakening her sexuality'. Presumably his own male sexuality has already been awakened – it was that sort of society – but Donne wrote early poems about this, in which he is more than grateful to the woman who has awakened him. In fact, at the beginning of the epithalamion he puts the bride and her groom firmly on an equal footing, by describing them as "you and your other you". And "tenderly/ The priest comes on his knees ..." To 'come' had a sexual sense to Donne, as it does to us.

It is impossible to defend anyone born before yesterday against accusations of political incorrectness. But surely, by any human standard, the passage quoted above is hardly the scene of bloody violence imagined by Davies or Carey. In fact, Donne is half-humorously turning the conventional 'scene of sacrifice' inside out.

The *Elegies* and *Satires* are all of a piece – to the extent that *Elegy* XIV, 'A Tale of A Citizen and his Wife', might as well be one of the *Satires*. A racy street story in rhymed iambic couplets, less formal than the five *Satires* (each of which takes a set theme: fashion, the law, religion, courtiers, and abuses of law at court), it makes fun of an uxorious citizen, his wife riding behind on the same horse, whom the poet, also on horseback, encounters on the road into London and attempts to chat up: his real interest is the citizen's wife who looks "well fitting for the feate" but who of course can say nothing, as conversation among strangers must be man to man. The citizen:

> Replies with onely yeas and nayes; At last
> (To fit his element) my theame I cast
> On Tradesmen's gaines; that set his tongue agoing,
> Alas, good sir (quoth he) There is no doing
> In Court nor City now; she smil'd, and I
> And (in my conscience) both gave him the lie
> In one met thought ...

As they part, the poet asks the citizen where he is staying, but the citizen is taciturn again:

> He barely named the street, promis'd the Wine,
> But his kinde wife gave me the very Signe.

That is, she not only spoke up at last and gave the poet the name of the inn at which they would be staying, but she made a gesture behind her husband's back. But Donne's way of treating it is more subtle than its cynicism would lead one to expect: "And (in my conscience) both gave him the lie/ In one met thought ..." They 'give him the lie' in the sense that they know there is plenty of "doing", even if he is not capable of doing it, and in the sense that they are thinking of 'lying' together. But are they? At the end, clearly, the wife invites the poet through a gesture. But earlier in the poem he is honest enough to mention his "conscience". Although the word brings in a hint of a religious conscience that is not in fact in evidence, its main meaning is 'awareness': he thinks the citizen's wife and he have "one met thought", but he could be deceiving himself ...

In almost any of the early 'cynical', promiscuous, etc. poems (critics have been great moralists with Donne), this subtle balance between satire – whose feeling is traditionally only scorn and contempt – and more tender or loving feelings, occurs. After all, "one met thought" is a lovely phrase. On another level (not necessarily a higher one: that is the beauty of the phrase) it is the theme of a later, very exalted poem, 'The Extasie'.

The *Elegies* seem to have been arranged in roughly chronological order, with the more serious ones (the Ann More ones, probably) towards the end, starting with XVI, the more flippant ones at the beginning. Here are 'Flavia' and 'Julia' and other figures in the Latinate tradition of Ovid's lightly satirical and superficial *Amores*, although Donne's intellectual bite suggests Propertius more than Ovid, and his combination of savagery and tenderness, Catullus. If there are stories, they are bedroom farces: the cuckolded husband snorting in his basket chair; the fear of being caught by "The grim eight-foot-high iron-bound serving-man,/ That oft names God in oathes and onely than"; the lover's betrayal to his mistress' (the unmarried one's) parents by the smell his "loud perfume", "base excrement of earth" (i.e. it may contain civet), leaves behind ...

But if they were only stories, even erotic ones, they would surely not offend some critics as they do. Donne, in his rebel with a cause phase, does make a thing of his and his mistress' right to choose what lovers they please. (It should be noted in passing that the word 'mistress' need not be taken as offensive: in Donne's day it had not developed the narrow sense of a married man's 'other woman', and was simply a polite word for a beloved woman – as in Shakespeare's "O mistress mine"). In an essay, 'On Women's Constancy' he had argued ingeniously that women had as much right to change lovers as men – it was only nature. And in poems such as *Elegy* III he took the same line:

> Women are made for men, not him, nor me,
> Foxes and goats; all beasts change, when they please,
> Shall women, more hot, wily, wild then these,
> Be bound to one man, and did Nature then
> Idly make then apter to endure then men?

And before this is read in a correct modern fashion as putting women down for being mere creatures of nature, shallow, etc, it is worth returning to that line:

> Women are made for men, not him, nor me.

He does not mean that women are unlike men in this. He is impressively willing to accept the consequences of women's freedom, to himself: women are made for men – not him, not me. In other words he is abjuring the right to monopolise, to 'own' a woman. His defiant (in *Elegy* XVII) "The heavens rejoice in motion, why should I/ Abjure my so much lov'd variety?" is a right he is willing to claim for women as much as for men.

It is evident from Donne's later poems that once he had found constancy with Ann More, he too became sexually possessive – and paid for this, as we all do. But it is worth making the point that his early celebrations of promiscuity were extremely courageous – and the more so because he was not merely flippant and superficial, like Ovid. He was much more like Catullus, who loved and adored his Lesbia ("mea Lesbia, Lesbia mea") even while she performs oral sex on (she glugs: "glubit") the descendants of Romulus in the doorways at every Roman crossroad. It is this appalling combination of cynicism and adoration, of the sense of a woman as a promiscuous animal capable of anything and as a person who is in herself worthy of worship, which offends the critics, so that the worthy editor C.A. Patrides can describe the *Elegies* as "aesthetically obscene".

The main offender is usually *Elegy* VIII, 'The Comparison', in which Donne compares his mistress, point by point, with a friend's. He begins with:

> ... the sweat drops of my Mistris breast,
> And on her necke her skin such lustre sets,
> They seeme no sweat drops, but pearle coronets.
> Rank sweaty froth thy Mistresse's brow defiles,
> Like spermatique issue of ripe menstruous boiles ...

and proceeds with similar hyperbole through parts of the body until he reaches his mistress' "best lov'd part". The passage is worth reading carefully:

> Then like the Chymicks masculine equal fire,
> Which in the Lymbecks warme wombe doth inspire

Into th'earth's worthless part a soule of gold,
Such cherishing heat her best lov'd part doth hold.
Thine's like the dread mouth of a fired gunne,
Or like hot liquid metalls newly runne
Into clay moulds, or like to that Aetna
Where round about the grasse is burnt away.

This is not quite a straightforward comparison: his own mistress'
parts are not actually described, while the friend's mistress' parts are
– the burnt away grass implying pubic hair around an erupting hole.
The comparison is not of the parts themselves but of how they are
treated: Donne sees himself as an alchemist engendering gold through
chemical reactions which cause the flask (the limbeck) to become
warm; his mistress' "part" is on the one hand "best lov'd" by him,
and on the other it contains "cherishing", i.e. loving, heat. In contrast,
his friend is not treating his mistress with love, not engendering gold,
nor is he cherished: instead he treats her, and her private parts like a
gun which he fires ('Fire' was an Elizabethan word for sperm). It is
this use which makes her parts into metal which 'runs' under forced
heat.

Donne continues very nastily with:

Are not your kisses then as filthy, and more,
As a worm sucking an invenomed sore?
Doth not thy fearfull hand in feeling quake,
As one which gath'ring flowers, still feares a snake?
Is not your last act harsh, and violent,
As when a Plough, a stony ground doth rent?

Each image is of a kind of activity in sex: first sucking as if eating
a poisonous exudate, then anxious and shaky groping, then harsh
and violent 'ploughing' of stony ground (a version of the biblical
images of ploughing the woman's land, as it were), and with a pun
on rent, which implies even further, firstly that the woman's vagina
is made into a gash by the aggressive cutting of the penis used like a
plough, and secondly that access to it has been paid for (i.e. she is a
whore).

By contrast:

So kisse good Turtles, so devoutly nice
Are Priests in handling reverent sacrifice,
And such in searching wounds the Surgeon is
As wee, when we embrace, or touch, or kisse.

This too has caused outrage: he is comparing his penis to a surgeon's probe, searching a wound – well, not exactly. He specifically says this applies not only in an "embrace", but when touching or kissing. He is saying that he is so gentle and neat ("nice") with his mistress in all his contact with her, that even if his penis or fingers or lips were as sharp as a surgeon's probe, his mistress would not be hurt. He is also reverent as a priest with a lamb (the same image as in the Lincoln's Inn Epithalamion). They are also, more conventionally, like turtle doves – associated with mutual billing and cooing. And, typically, he repeats for emphasis the "we": this is something they are both doing.

All this follows the comparison of the two mistress' "parts". And what he is saying, translated into prose, is something like: my mistress' vagina is warm and engendering of golden feelings, because I treat it and her reverently and devotedly as she treats me, in a mutual act; your mistress's vagina is like a fired gun or a volcanic rent surrounded by scorched grass, because you fuck her, perpetrate an act on her, in a harsh and violent way.

This is not an unsubtle thought. And it was not until the 20th century and Wilhelm Reich's *The Function of the Orgasm* that scientific psychology began to look at the different ways in which people actually behave in sex, and how harsh and violent movements may produce a technical climax and a sense of relief, but not a deeply-felt orgasm.

Donne concludes his poem abruptly:

Leave her, and I will leave comparing thus,
She, and comparisons are odious.

In other words: stop treating your mistress like this, and I'll stop comparing her with my mistress; your treatment has made your mistress so odious, I don't even wish to think of her and my mistress as being the same kind of creature. Ugly much of the poem may be, but it is not, after all, cynical.

In *Elegy* II, 'The Anagram', which has been found similarly offensive, Donne makes a similar point about "parts":

> Though all her parts be not in th'usuall place,
> She hath yet an Anagram of a good face.

In other words, beauty is in the eye of the beholder: it is a question of how the parts are integrated by the eye which can give meaning even to a jumble of features by re-arranging them. Again, Donne is celebrating inconstancy, flux even: his view of the world is never static, always dynamic.

Some of the *Songs and Sonets*, especially an apparent cluster which appears near the end of this section of the 1635 edition, seem to have been written contemporaneously with the early *Elegies*, and celebrate inconstancy with the same frantic vigour. These poems – 'Negative Love', 'The Prohibition', 'The Computation', 'The Paradox', 'Farewell to Love', 'Love's Diet' – read as if they could have been written to anyone, are at times intellectual without feeling, and revel in witty paradox, especially about "dying" and "lying" in their sexual senses. "Can a ghost die?" "Wee dye but once, and who lov'd last did die,/ Hee that saith twice, doth lye." But 'The Expiration', which is placed among the poems listed above, and belongs with them in its witty playing with the 'dying' theme, begins with a sudden note of tenderness:

> So, so, break off this last lamenting kisse,
> Which sucks two soules, and vapors Both away ...

The poem is about a parting which follows so close on orgasm that it causes a double death. It concludes with a play on the sexual sense of the word 'go' (which the Elizabethans used in this context as they used 'come'), as the lover tells his beloved to go, and feels he is dying from this, as at the same time he is 'going':

> Except it be too late, to kill me so,
> Being double dead, going, and bidding, goe.

It would seem that Donne was becoming hooked: on the evidence even of the poems which celebrate inconstancy, he had a dangerous

26

tendency to become involved. Another poem of parting, *Elegy* V, 'His Picture' – which must predate his relationship with Ann More, because it is about his setting off on a military expedition – begins:

> Here take my Picture; though I bid farewell;
> Thine in my heart, where my soule dwells, shall dwell ...

And the poem goes on to reason, hopefully, that when he returns from the wars, "My body'a sack of bones, broken within,/ And powder's blew staines scatter'd on my skinne", his beloved can refer to the picture for evidence of how "fair and delicate" he was before – and decide that after all she prefers him in his altered state, that she will have developed a taste for "what seemes tough". It is a poem by a man in love, but more than this, of a man with some sense of his own and his mistress' character, their ways of reasoning.

In the end Donne seems to have been hoist on his own petard. Or, he who lives by the sword dies by the sword ... Clichés come to mind, as they did to Donne's in some poems at the time because having started his very own sexual revolution – not simply by having affairs, like many other swivers at Lincoln's Inn, but by making a creed of having them – he counted consequences which were inevitably banal. First one of the probably two women with whom he so devotedly celebrated inconstancy, but for whom feelings of constancy began to emerge, seems to have lived up to his expectations and dumped him harshly for another man. In 'A Jeat Ring Sent' he concludes:

> She that, Oh, broke her faith, would soon break thee.

And although the Elizabethans worked the theme of the 'scornful mistress' from cliché to cliché, there is a real howl of pain when Donne writes about it in 'The Apparition':

> When by thy scorne, O Murdresse, I am dead ...

But, characteristically, he goes further into his feelings than a howl, in turning the usual betrayed lover's obsessive musings about what his former mistress may be doing now with a new lover, into a carefully observed picture of what his ghost will see when he spies on her, "feigned vestall" – i.e. she has pretended to be a virgin – in "worse armes" than his. Already the new lover – or more likely husband, given the crack about "feigned vestall" – will be fed up with her sexual demands:

> ... he, whose thou art then, being tyr'd before,
> Will, if thou stirre, or pinch to wake him, thinke
> > Thou call'st for more,
> And in false sleepe will from thee shrinke ...

Yes, this is nasty. But it is not nastiness for its own sake. Donne is willing to face, in the poem (and expose to the potential reader) his own obsessively detailed revenge fantasy – which, in the end, is pathetic. He goes on:

> What I will say, I will not tell thee now,
> Lest that preserve thee ...

And suddenly the lack of detail turns his remark into an empty threat. It is like King Lear's "I will do such things,/ What they are I know not; but they shall be/ The terrors of the earth." The rage is intense, but impotent.

Other poems which treat betrayal are 'Love's Deitie', 'The Message', and 'The Will', in which the mistress "thinkes her friendship a fit portion/ For yonger lovers". It seems that in fact both mistresses betrayed him: the unmarried one through marriage in which she feigned virginity, and the married one through seeking other lovers. *Elegy* VII states that although this mistress was married (perhaps to the old geezer in the basket chair – speculatively, Mr Parvish), she was "nature's lay Ideot". This is interpreted accurately by Patrides to mean that she was an "ignorant uninitiate in the workings of nature", but no doubt the odd use of the word 'lay' is no accident: although a child of nature, she did not know much about what is still called in America a 'lay'.

"I taught thee to love", Donne states, "and in that sophistrie, Oh, thou dost prove/ Too subtile". Poor Donne. His mistress has learned with him how to enjoy sex, and is now trying her skills elsewhere. He can see the humour of it, and even attempts to wrangle the argument that since he has "refin'd" her "into a blis-full paradise", she is still really his. But he does not believe this, and finishes in a flurry of boasts which are so clichéd he must know they are empty.

In *Elegy* XII, in the midst of atypical comedy scene (one thinks of Jonson's plays) about adultery, Donne finally comes out with what he really values: 'Constancie':

> Was't not enough, that thou didst hazard us
> To paths in love so dark, so dangerous:
> And those so ambush'd round with household spies,
> And over all thy husbands towring eyes
> That flam'd with oylie sweat of jealousie,
> Yet went we not still on with Constancie?

In spite of his boast in *Elegy* VII, "I taught thee to love", it seems the truth may have also worked the other way: Donne's mistresses also taught him to love. He delighted with them in the changefulness of sex for its own sake, but when they – as his theory of inconstancy had predicted quite cheerfully – moved on to other lovers, he was left with a terrible sadness. This is expressed in what seems to be the first of his four *Valediction Poems*, 'A Valediction of my name, in the window'. He is parting from a mistress whom he knows will be tempted into intrigues ("thy melted maid,/ Corrupted by thy Lover's gold, and page,/ His letter at thy pillow hath laid …") and will almost certainly give in to them. His only hope is that she will restrain herself by looking at his name, engraved with a diamond on her window pane. But, with his usual thinking through to the end, he is chagrined that such a strategy is even necessary:

> But glasse, and lines must bee,
> No meanes our firme substantiall love to keepe ...

And in the end he gives up:

> Impute this idle talke, to that I goe,
> For dying men talk often so.

3 Platonic Love

Donne grew up in a rigid scheme of things: Catholicism, which in turn depended intellectually on Aristotelianism, which in turn depended on Platonism. All believe in an underlying, essential order. This order Donne rebelliously rejected, in his Lincoln's Inn days, in favour of a kind of Heraclitean flux such as had preceded Plato. But not being a fool, he was aware of his own craving for what he had rejected. This appears in the *Satires*. It is, again, something of a cliché – part of history, rather than poetry – that the satirist is a social conservative. He explicitly harangues society for its failings to live up to an implicit order.

Some critics have supposed that Donne wrote *Satires* (as now numbered) 1 and 2, then 4 and 5 in the 1590s, but *Satire* 3 – on religion – in 1620 or so, after he had been ordained. There is no convincing internal evidence for this. And it presupposes first that Donne, in his rebellious youth, had totally shelved that part of his mind which was concerned with religion, and second that after ordination, and Ann's death, when he had no more use for poetry, he was capable of sitting down and writing a *Satire* in the vein of those youthful ones he would rather officially have forgotten.

More likely, he embarked on these set pieces in youthful ambitiousness to cover the main fields of activity in the world he knew: the court, religion, and law. It is not even necessary to suppose that he waited until he worked for Egerton before writing the law satire. For once in his work, we seem to have a set of poems written in a genre, at roughly the same time, the early 1590s when Donne was carried away, like many young poets, with the possibilities of sheer verse – because, strictly speaking, although written with verve, the *Satires* are not inspired. Not to worry: Dryden and Pope in the 'Age of Obsequiousness' brought so-called poetry to the state of a totally cerebral and calculated art, through satires in rhymed couplets. They considered Donne barbarous. It is this barbarity – rough rather than smooth – which makes his *Satires* more readable in our day than Dryden's or Pope's. In the lack of knowledge of what Latin poetry actually sounded like, it is hard to say if Donne's (and Dryden's and Pope's) model, Juvenal, was rough or smooth. But, like Juvenal,

Donne devoted his *Satires* to a general attack on hypocrisy in each of the areas he treated. Although his ridiculous social climber, in *Satire* 1, may for all we know be based on an acquaintance, he did not have the bad taste to lampoon by name or pseudonym, as Dryden or Pope did, the pretentious nonentities of his day.

The prosody of the *Satires* has been considered difficult by critics lulled to sleep by too much 19th century rocking-of-the-cradle metre, or turned off metre altogether by the chopped prose effect of 20th century free verse. Perhaps we are now free again, simply to read the *Satires* aloud, conversationally, and take them as they come. For example the beginning of *Satire* IV:

> Well; I may now receive, and die; My sinne
> Indeed is great, but I have beene in
> A Purgatorie, such as fear'd hell is
> A recreation to, and scant map of this.
> My minde, neither with prides itch, nor yet hath been
> Poyson'd with love to see, or to bee scene,
> I had no suit there, nor new suite to shew,
> Yet went to Court ...

The trick here, as with all Donne's verse, is to take the punctuation as dramatic: if there is no comma there is no pause, if there is one there is a short pause, and if there is a semi-colon a longer one, and a full-stop the longest one. An apostrophe, as in "though'it", reminds us to read as one syllable.

For the modern reader the problem with the *Satires* is more likely to be in their allusions. Put simply, most of us make love (or 'have sex'), so Donne's poems on sex, even if they look at it in a new way, do not present such a stream of local references. The *Satires* are for the most part not poetry, in which intensity of emotion tends to keep focus on physical reality, but verse, which is as free as prose to digress into all sorts of topical and local references. Broadly speaking, there is a hierarchy of difficulty in Donne's work. The *Elegies*, *Epigrams*, and *Songs and Sonets* are the least difficult: although they compress infinitely more meaning into a few lines than his other work, this is the nature of inspired poems, and we are so taken emotionally by them that their different levels of meaning either strike us right away or compel us to careful study. The *Divine Poems* are somewhat more difficult because, at least if we live in the UK where less than 20 percent of people bother with church, their allusions are unfamiliar and need to be looked up. Still more difficult are the *Satires*, the 'Verse Letters' and other longer, artificial set pieces such as the 'Anniversaries', because they are more like prose, more topical and local, and not compelling as poetry, so the incentive to look things up in a dictionary or history book is further reduced. And most difficult are the prose works and sermons, on which few modern readers can keep their minds, because they are rife with allusions to matters which do not concern us, and because the form of prose has changed more than poetry over 400 years: Robert Graves' lyric 'Despite and Still' ("Have you not heard/ The words in my head ...?") and Donne's 'Song' ("Sweetest love I do not go/ For weariness of thee ...") could almost be interchanged in time. But a passage of Graves' expository prose, say in one of his *Oxford Addresses on Poetry*, is infinitely easier to read than one of Donne's *Sermons*: the respective sentence structures and lengths differ enormously, and the comparative lack of verbs in Donne's prose (though not in his poetry, which is packed with them: we know this, because Theodore Redpath has counted them ...) is disconcerting.

The *Satires*, then, insofar as they resemble prose rather than poetry, can be difficult to follow. They are worth the effort, though, since they paint a picture of a social world which was not painted by anyone else – not even Shakespeare, although he described other things. Donne's *Satire* 1, for example, gives a flavour of what it must have been like to walk on a London street with a maniac social climber, in 1595 or so:

> Now leaps he upright, Joggs me, and cryes, Do you see
> Yonder well favoured youth? Which? Oh, 'tis hee
> That dances so divinely; Oh, said I,
> Stand still, must you dance here for company?
> Hee droopt, wee went, till one (which did excell
> Th'Indians, in drinking his Tobacco well)
> Met us; they talk'd; I whispered, let'us goe,
> 'T may be you smell him not, truely I doe;
> He heares not mee, but, on the other side
> A many-coloured Peacock having spide,
> Leaves him and mee ...

The pace of this is like that of the Mel Brooks film *High Anxiety* in which Brooks and the mad-looking Marty Feldman strut frenetically through the craziness of Hollywood ... It is not surprising that the *Satires* were written at the same time as the poems of inconstancy: they describe Heraclitean flux, and Donne, although at times an invisible narrator, has clearly had enough of it.

The *Epigrams*, also written early, are mainly witty rather than profound, but like the epigrams of the Roman poet Martial from which they ultimately derive, they include flashes of poetry and of compressed insight, as in 'A selfe accuser', which rings autobiographically:

> Your mistris, that you follow whores, still taxeth you:
> 'Tis strange that she should thus confesse it, though' it be true.

Ben Jonson also wrote epigrams (as he also wrote Ovidian elegies, although these are flaccid stuff compared to Donne's: he was at his best in songs and lyrics) which, like Donne's were greatly admired. But an epigram, witty and brief, is easily admired by people with not much sense for poetry, and for serious poets it is likely to represent a sudden flash of thought, of not much consequence. Donne only wrote 20 of them, some classical, like 'Niobe':

> By childrens births, and death, I am become
> So dry, that I am now my own sad tombe.

Others, like 'Antiquary' might as well be couplets from the *Satires*:

> If in his Studie he hath so much care
> To hang all old strange things, let his wife beware.

But it was the *Epigrams* about incidents Donne had observed on military expeditions which excited most praise. 'A burnt ship' and 'Fall of a Wall' have already been quoted from: they were much admired but they are essentially cold – an example of what Donne's poetry would have all been like if he had not been inspired by emotion: merely clever.

Much more than clever, though not openly emotional, are the two verse letters Donne wrote to Christopher Brooke (who was later imprisoned for acting as Donne's best man at the secret wedding to Ann) either during or soon after his sea voyage to the Azores in 1597: 'The Storme' and 'The Calme'. These are described by Patrides as "rigorously classical", and they are reminiscent of descriptive passages from Virgil, as if taken out of context. But they are quite new in English, and there was a gap of almost 200 years before the early romantic interest in natural phenomena led to similar descriptions in poems by Crabbe and Wordsworth. They are of particular interest in the light of the struggle in Donne between inconstancy and constancy, in his love life at the time. What could be more inconstant than a storm, more constant than a calm? One senses his fascination with these two extremes – and ultimately, his impatience with them. He even makes the link overtly between the impersonal events of the elements at sea, and the intimate events he had left behind in London. (He never seems to have been far from London in his mind). In 'The Storme' he describes men who peeping fearfully out of their cabins:

> And tremblingly'aske what newes, and doe heare so,
> Like jealous husbands, what they would not know.

And in 'The Calme' he writes:

> Smooth as thy mistresse glasse, or what shines there,
> The sea is now.

It was probably at this time, when his Lincoln's Inn phase was ending with disillusion and betrayal, and before his York House phase in which he would meet Ann More and find new hope, that Donne seems to have tried to go down another path: that of platonic love, with Magdalen Herbert. The evidence for this is first from the biographical account by Walton of Donne's friendship (according to Walton not one "that polluted their Souls") with Magdalen Herbert at this time, and secondly from poems which have been traditionally (as recorded in glosses or notes by contemporaries) associated with her: 'The Autumnal', 'The Primrose', and 'The Relique'. As noted earlier, 'The Blossome' is almost certainly a companion to 'The Primrose'. 'The Funerall' is a companion to 'The Relique'. And another poem which, from its uncharacteristic theme, probably belongs with these is 'The Untertaking', titled in some manuscripts, 'Platonique Love'.

Some biographers (e.g. Bald) take Walton's view that Donne met Mrs Herbert when she lived in Oxford for a year, 1599-1600. Donne would have visited friends there, including Mrs Herbert's son Edward. Others (e.g. Parker) assume he first met her earlier, when she visited London. Walton was, like his younger contemporary, John Aubrey, a master of anecdote, but his dates are often demonstrably muddled. Parker's view is more consistent with a timing of Donne's relationship with Mrs Herbert as suggested above. He probably first met Ann briefly at York House in 1597, when she was only 14 (he was 25) and it is unlikely they became lovers, but after this meeting it is also unlikely that Donne would have been inclined to practise platonic love with Mrs Herbert and when this rather quickly failed, to threaten, as he does in 'The Blossome', to go back to London "to another friend, whome wee shall finde/ As glad to have my body as my minde."

'The Autumnal' is a weird poem to find among the *Elegies*, of which it is number IX. It is cluttered with abstractions in italics, beginning:

> No Spring, nor *Summer* Beauty hath such grace,
> As I have seen in one *Autumnall* face ...

and after equally formal discursion about "*Affections*" and "*Reverences* name", it arrives at:

> Call not these wrinkles, graves: If graves they were,
> They were *Loves graves;* for else he is no where ...

And later:

> Here, where still *Evening is;* not noone nor night;
> Where no *voluptuousnesse,* yet all *delight* ...

The formality, from Donne of all people, is striking. And although he is always capable of showing off and being flash, there is an unusual note here of parading learning for its own sake, and of sententiousness. He is obviously trying to impress, and with his puns on being "grave" he is even trying to seem older than he is: 25 at most. And the "autumnal" Magdalen Herbert, wrinkles and all, is aged at the time – 32! Although much is made of Elizabethan women 'ageing early' because of childbirth (Mrs Herbert eventually had 10 children), portraits of them, and poems inspired by them even when they were middle-aged, belie this: it was an age in which those who survived to adulthood were tough but not necessarily unbeautiful or without sexual passion. Donne's own mother married three times, and Mrs Herbert, as mentioned earlier, married when she was over 40 a man half her age, Sir John Danvers, who was ardently devoted to her until she died at 58.

However, it seems that a sexual relationship with Donne was 'not on'. Whether this was as much his wish as hers, or he was simply making a virtue of necessity, he did – as always – believe in what he was doing. 'The Undertaking' or 'Platonique Love' is a remarkable statement of its subject:

> I have done one braver thing
> Then all the Worthies did,
> And yet a braver thence doth spring,
> Which is, to keep that hid ...
>
> If, as I have, you also doe
> Vertue'atired in women see,
> And dare love that, and say so too,
> And forget the Hee and Shee ...

Again in 'The Primrose' he says:

> I walk to find a true Love; and I see
> That 'tis not a mere woman, that is shee,
> But must, or more, or lesse then women bee ...

This seems a knotty statement, but means just what it says: he is seeking a woman who is in a sense not a woman – either she is more than woman, when she is divine, or less than woman, when she does not act sexually as "shee." Moreover, to be woman is not in fact "lesse" than being divine, so that to be divine is both more or less than woman. His subsequent reasoning about how the primrose, as representative of women ("women, whom this flower doth represent")

36

must "thrive" with her "true number five" – it is five petalled, star-like, and to be "true", exactly itself as it were, cannot have either four or six petals – makes the same point. All this is very Platonic, in that it seeks the "true" woman who is behind the actual one. And Aristotelian, in that it treats of essences. And Petrarchan ...

More importantly, however, 'The Primrose' is a poem about poetry and about a more ancient tradition than the Platonic one: the tradition of 'Our Lady of the Wild Things', the identity of woman and nature, and the poet's Muse. Robert Graves contentedly discussed 'The Primrose' in his book on this tradition, *The White Goddess*. (And in more detail in one of his Clarke lectures, 1953). Without becoming mystical about it, it is safe to say that in this poem Donne is trying to make Magdalen Herbert (who lived at Montgomery Castle on the 'Primrose Hill' the poem describes) into something other than herself: a Muse figure to whom he can write poems even though he cannot physically have her. This sense of intellectual effort – as in 'The Autumnal' he is trying to live up to her intellectual expectations of him – has led some critics to call the poem cold. And so it would be, if it were merely a statement of Muse doctrine.

But it is not. Poetry being poetry, even when the poet is trying hard to believe in an ideal – even the ideal of the Muse, of woman as a perfect star, a five-petalled flower – the truth will out, whether the poet likes it or not. And the truth in this case is that Magdalen Herbert is not a perfect five, as it were: she is precisely that 4 or 6, that more or less than woman, whom Donne simultaneously does and does not want her to be. Because she is "above/ All thought of sexe", and she "thinks to move" Donne's heart "to study her, and not to love" – he makes an artificial Muse out of her. How is this made clear? By another level of the poem – its 'subtext' as the deconstructionists would say. Woman's "sexe", her vagina, has for centuries of poetry been represented as a rose. But this poem is about a primrose – a prim rose, a prim woman.

The word is assumed to originate from 'prime rose', i.e. the first rose or flower of Spring – which is, as Donne sees it, fertilised, as it were, by the early rains:

> Upon this Primrose Hill
> Where, if Heav'n would distill

> A shoure of raine, each severall drop might goe
> To his owne primrose, and grow Manna so ...

Hardly a cold beginning. Primroses had a sexual connotation for the Elizabethans, as in Hamlet's line about "the primrose path of dalliance". 'Heaven' was used by the Elizabethans (see Shakespeare's *Sonnet* 129) to mean a woman's vagina, or more precisely the prospect of it. Donne is saying that the prospect of his woman's vagina will bring out moisture on his penis (his own primrose, in that it will 'prime' the vagina), and form a new life-giving substance, a Manna. And it is not out of order to suggest that Donne is also making a double pun on 'man' and perhaps jokingly 'manner' – i.e. becoming more of a man (his 'man' becoming more erect) and a 'manner' in that his semen makes men (in the broad biblical sense of 'people').

Robert Graves was right to incorporate 'The Primrose' into the tradition of the 'Muse poem'. But he missed the point. As so often in poems which idealistically follow a Muse formula (as too many of Graves' own late poems did), the Muse gets her revenge, as it were, by slipping in the truth. The poet should be grateful. We cannot know what Donne felt about his own poem beyond what it says about itself. He started out to make his 'prime rose', on her very own hill, into an ideal, and did indeed make a powerful statement of that ideal – but realised in the poem that Magdalen Herbert was not a prime rose, but a prim one. The poem is complex because it is saying at the same time that his beloved 'true' woman is neither more nor less than a woman – but that insofar as she is 'above sex', she is after all both more and less ... It is not surprising that in 'The Blossome', probably written shortly afterwards, he resolves to head back to London where he can be loved for his body, not his mind.

He seems to have been left in the state of mind – he did, after all, still have a mind – of 'The Funerall' and 'The Relique', the two poems about his corpse with a bracelet of hair around the arm. In 'The Funerall' it is "That subtile wreath of haire, which crownes my arme". He claims "this mystery" is his "outward Soule" which will protect his limbs from "dissolution" (pun no doubt intended: the prim Magdalen's gift of the hair bracelet will have prevented him from baring himself in "dissolution" with other women), but eventually his sense of humour has taken over and he is posing as a martyr, then abruptly switches to the killer statement: "since you would have none of nice, I bury some of you."

In 'The Relique' , he is not being shrouded for burial, his grave is actually being dug up, "some second ghest to entertaine", and the diggers spot (in that wonderful line) "a bracelet of bright haire about the bone". This is the one of the pair of poems that gives the clue that they are to Magdalen Herbert, since he develops further the idea from 'The Funerall' that he will be venerated as a martyr and adds that:

> ... he that digges us up, will bring
> Us, to the Bishop, and the King,
> To make us Reliques; then
> Thou shalt be a Mary Magdalen, and I
> A something else thereby ...

Mary Magdalen is noted in the bible for her hair – and according to some commentators may have been a hairdresser, and to other commentators a prostitute. Elizabethan pronunciation is not certain, but one of its successors is Northern Irish, in which the words 'whore' and 'hair' are pronounced the same, to rhyme with 'fur'. Donne was not incapable of having a laugh in this poem, even in the beautiful line "a bracelet of bright hair about the bone". Mary Magdalen may have been a "bright whore" (which Donne would not have meant disrespectfully). And if the reader finds this suggestion (which admittedly depends on a conjecture about pronunciation) too outrageous, he or she might still consider the fact that in some dialects of English, a frequent word for an erection is 'boner'. The powerful sexual imagery of the "bracelet of bright hair about the bone" does not escape readers and critics. But it is on one level a serious sexual image, and on another a humorous one. This is one of Donne's main characteristics: that he is serious and humorous at the same time. It gets him into trouble: when puritans are offended by the grossness of a scene like the one in the 'Epithalamion' where the lover priest prepares to "embowell" his bride, Donne's ghost cannot protest that he meant it as a joke – because he also meant it seriously. (Although, as noted, the word "embowell" is not so gross as it seems.)

'The Relique' ends on a pious and unhumorous note, as Donne says that:

Difference of sex no more we knew,
Then our Guardian Angells doe ...

... These miracles wee did; but now alas,
All measure, and all language, I should prise,
Should I tell what a miracle shee was.

And in spite of his jokes, his attempts to distance himself from his pain, he probably did believe Magdalen Herbert was a miracle – literally something which is seen (from Latin 'mirare'), a vision. In 'Platonique Love' he mentions "the skill of specular stone", referring (according to Patrides) to selenite which in *Sermon* VII he described as "transparent as glasse, or crystall". Magdalen Herbert was not known for beauty – which after his early experiences Donne may not have been looking for – but she was known for her intelligence, which must have had a kind of clarity. Perhaps Donne was horrified that, after all, he desired her. At any rate, his 'Platonic Love' ended in pain – just like physical love. 'The Autumnal' had in fact predicted this, at the end, when suddenly after over 40 lines of abstractions, comes a blunt statement: "I hate extreames" – 'The Storme' and 'The Calme' again? – and the conclusion:

… yet I had rather stay
With Tombs, then Cradles, to weare out a day.
Since such loves motion natural is, may still
My love descend, and journey downe the hill,
Not panting after growing beauties, so,
I shall ebbe out with them, who home-ward goe.

4   Poems of Constancy

Suddenly, in the *Elegies* as printed in the 1635 order, the tone changes
with *Elegy* XVI (subtitled in one manuscript, 'His wife would have
gone as his Page'):

> By our first strange and fatall interview,
> By all desires which thereof did ensue,
> By our long starving hopes, by that remorse
> Which my words masculine perswasive force
> Begot in thee, and by the memory
> Of hurts, which spies and rivals threatened me,
> I calmly beg. But by thy fathers wrath,
> By all parties, which want and divorcement hath,
> I conjure thee, and all the oathes which I
> And thou have sworne to scale joynt constancy,
> Here I unswear and overswear them thus,
> Thou shalt not love by ways so dangerous ...

He goes on to dissuade his "true mistris" from her plan to accompany him into exile disguised as his page – this is the meaning of
those lines about the "indifferent" Italians who might lust after her
thinking she is a boy, which have so enraged correct modern critics.
This must be Ann, only 17 years old, slim as a boy, and in the fuss of
having been discovered as Donne's love. It would seem from the
poem that her father and others, although they would want to disallow
or "divorce" their secret marriage if they knew about it, do not in
fact yet know all. There is still some possibility of concealment.
(The history of Donne's marriage starts with its discovery: how this
came about is not documented). Perhaps to avoid being thrown in
prison as in fact he was, Donne seems to have entertained the idea of
fleeing to Italy:

> When I am gone, dreame me some happinesse,
> Nor let thy lookes our long hid love confesse,
> Nor praise, nor dispraise me, nor blesse nor curse
> Openly loves force, nor in bed fright thy Nurse
> With midnight startings, crying out, oh, oh,
> Nurse, o my love is slaine, I saw him goe

41

O'r the white Alpes alone; I saw him I,
Assail'd, fight, taken, stabb'd, bleed, fall, and die ...

Melodramatic perhaps, but there is a new pulse of emotion here,
and a quality which can be associated with all Donne's poems which
seem to be to Ann: an entering into her mind, a speaking of her
language. "When by thy scorne, O Murdresse, I am dead": in his
earlier poems there is a formal distance, in spite of the sexual relationship, between Donne and his mistress. Now there is a closeness.
And, in this poet who prided himself in being "harsh" and has been
considered by critics as such, a sudden appearance of an extraordinary beauty:

... Thou hast reade
How roughly bee in pieces shivered
Fair Orithea,whom he swore he lov'd ...

Other *Elegies* (which may have been written earlier than the
discovery of Donne and Ann's relationship in 1601) oscillate between
inconstancy and constancy, but now constancy always wins. *Elegy*
XVII, the one which starts with the question "Why should I/ Abjure
my so much lov'd variety ... ?" concludes that:

... beauty with true worth securely weighing,
Which being found assembled in some one
Wee'l leave her ever, and love her alone.

Elegies XVIII, XIX, and XX – the famous 'Loves Progresse',
'To his Mistress Going to Bed', and 'Loves Warre', in which the
final peace is signed in the battle between the sexes – are also
obviously to Ann. 'Loves Warre' ends:

But stay swords, armes, and shott
To make at home; And shall I not do then
More glorious service, staying to make men?

'Make love not war!' Donne is in character as a rebel here, 360
years before a popular slogan emerged expressing the same idea.
And now he takes up more seriously than in his "Manna" reference
in 'The Primrose' the possibility of making men – meaning human

beings – a task on which he and Ann were embarked. But, as always, although now carried away with joy, Donne does not stop thinking. While, in 'To his Mistress Going to Bed' celebrating "full nakedness!" and encouraging his somewhat timid mistress to "as liberally, as to a Midwife shew/ Thy selfe: cast all, yea, this white lynnen hence ...", he is careful to assert equality: "What needst thou have more covering then a man." In 'Loves Progresse' he provides an intricate argument for starting caresses at the woman's feet and working upward, rather than starting at the face and working down – a humorous argument, it must be noted in order to allay the possible wrath of the modern Thought Police – then cannot resist trying to clarify a distinction he had worked on in 'The ["aesthetically obscene"] Comparison':

> ... But if we
> Make love to woman; virtue is not she:
> As beauty'is not, nor wealth: He that strayes thus
> From her to hers, is more adulterous,
> Then if he took her maid.

This is an extraordinarily profound statement which should be hung up on everyone's wall. To rephrase it in approximate and longwinded prose: if we men make love to women, we may well tell ourselves it is because they are specially virtuous, or specially beautiful, or specially rich. But if we think this way, we are straying from the woman herself to some quality of hers. It is the same if we stray to her vagina as something she has – "hers" – rather than simply to her. If we stray from loving her as her, in her whole self, and instead love what is hers – her virtue, her beauty, her money – we are committing adultery: we are being unfaithful to her in straying to hers. What is hers might as well be a separate person: if we want her vagina, say, in itself – rather than all of her – we might as well want the vagina of another woman. Her maid, for example. (Who in turn, by the logic of my argument, would be betrayed if I made love to hers rather than her). But I use my beloved woman's maid as an example, because in a punning sense she is 'made'. If I do not take the woman I love as a whole – as her – in taking "hers" I am manufacturing a version of her: a woman's virtue, her beauty, her wealth are all 'made' attributes. A woman is not her attributes, she is herself.

The phrase is in fact part of a sustained argument which has begun with the injunction: "preferr/ one woman first, and then one thing in her". In other words, before admiring her attributes ("hers"), admire her as a whole self. In the argument he remarks:

> Can men more injure women then to say
> They love them for that, by which they're not they?

This prefigures the "her to hers" phrase. In other words, men are actually insulting women when they compliment them for their attributes: women want to be loved for themselves.

And Donne is anathema to feminist critics! He is making a much more subtle psychological point than the one made in 'The Comparison', although on the same track. He must have learned it from Ann – not necessarily verbally, but through his relationship with her.

We know almost nothing about Ann More. Bald remarks patronisingly that she was "a devout girl", but cites no evidence. She wrote no letters which survive. But she must have known how to think, as well as to feel. Her presence permeates all Donne's poems from the moment he met her (excepting only the *Divine Poems*, although a reflection of her presence enters into them too), and the most famous, 'Batter my heart', is nothing less than an attempt to enlist God's aid in freeing Donne from her power over him. (Verse letters to friends, eulogies to female patrons, obsequies to the illustrious dead – all Donne's attempts at public verse – are not, by the standards of Donne's love poems, poems at all.)

Although in the usual order of Donne's poems following the 1635 edition, the *Elegies* which must be to Ann are at the end (XVI to XX), as fits the chronology, the reverse is broadly true of the *Songs and Sonets*: whoever ordered them seems to have put the poems to Ann at the beginning. Although they are mixed in with some poems on the usual theme of inconstancy – such as the famous 'Song' which begins "Goe, and catch a falling starre" (irremediably contaminated for anyone alive in the 1950s by the crooner Perry Como's slushy hit, "Catch a falling star, and put it in your pocket, keep it for a rainy day ...") – they stand out for a difference in mood which has emerged in the *Elegies* to Ann. In a word, they are happy.

Who could not take pleasure in:

> Busie old foole, unruly Sunne
> Why dost thou thus
> Through windows, and through curtaines call on us?
> Must to thy motions lovers seasons run?

Any young lover feels a complicity with this rejection of busy old fools, and with the grand selfishness of:

> She is all States, and all Princes, I,
> Nothing else is ...

and the conclusion:

> This bed thy centre is, these walls, thy spheare.

Donne writes a lot about 'spheares' in these poems to Ann, and a lot about angels – which were pronounced with a short 'A': Ann-gels. The 'g' was probably soft, as it is now – as in 'danger'. But there is some possibility it was hard – as in 'anger'. If so, 'angell' would sound the same as 'Ann girl' (in the traditional pronunciation of 'girl' as 'gel') which adds another dimension to this pun.

Donne relishes the idea of drawing all his and his mistress' existence into the 'spheare' of their possession of each other. The 'spheare' may even be as tiny as 'The Flea' in which their "two bloods mingled bee." Or as in 'The good-morrow', the lovers can be the two "hemispheares" of one world: "let us possesse one world, each hath one, and is one."

In the over-flowing happiness of 'The good-morrow', Donne wrote:

> If ever any beauty I did see,
> Which I desir'd, and got, t'was but a dreame of thee.

Perhaps this idea bothered him: why think of past loves now? Or, in light-heartedly reassuring his new love that his past affairs had been mere anticipatory dreams of the real thing, as it were, with her, did he wonder if he was deceiving himself? The famously difficult 'Aire and Angels' straightens this problem out on a high and serious level:

Twice or thrice had I loved thee
Before I knew thy face or name;
So in a voice, so in a shapeless flame,
Angells affect us oft, and worship'd bee,
  Still when, to where thou wert, I came
Some lovely glorious nothing I did see,
  But since, my soule, whose child love is,
Takes limmes of flesh, and else could nothing doe,
  More subtile than the parent is,
Love must not be, but take a body too,
  And therefore what thou wert, and who
    I did Love aske, and now
That it assume thy body, I allow,
And fix it selfe in thy lip, eye, and brow.

Donne is taking up the issue of how his fulfilment with his true love has been prefigured, in part, in two or three relationships he has had earlier: he implies that in his moments of pleasure with these previous loves he had sensed something missing which he has now found. The poem only becomes difficult when "Angells" are brought in. But this is logical: what has been missing with other women cannot be merely physical parts. This is the 'her, not hers' theme of *Elegy* XVIII. Ann's essence (the more so since she is an 'anngel') is, if considered apart from her physical attributes, as Donne wants to consider it, a "lovely glorious nothing". Patrides' note on this line refers the reader to 'Negative Love' (one of Donne's poems of inconstancy) which begins:

I never stoop'd so low, as they
Which on an eye, cheeke, lip, can prey ...

Again the 'her not hers' theme. It is not necessary to get caught in the intricacies of the Renaissance debates about whether Angels had a physical substance. Donne appears to believe they do not. But he and Ann do. In one of his early *Paradoxes,* number 6, 'That the gifts of the body are better than those of the mind or of fortune', he had set his view out clearly:

My body liceneceth my Soule to let the Worlds beauties
through mine eyes, to heare pleasant things through my eares,

and affords it apt Organs for conveyance of all perceivable
delights. But alas my Soule cannot make any part, that is not
of it selfe disposed, to see and heare ...

He is wrangling, quite perversely, the point that since the soul
depends on the body while it is in it, in order to perceive the world,
this gives the body the upper hand, as it were: unless the body's
parts are "disposed" (i.e. willing, as if they have a mind of their own,
as well as apt or suitable in their design), the soul cannot perceive.
He never was able to resolve this question in prose. It even bothers
him in his sermons, where his only means of trying to resolve it is to
look ahead to the Last Judgement and assert that at least then, soul
and body will be one. But the question does resolve itself in poetry,
because unlike prose it can contain even within the same statement
seemingly opposing truths. If 'Aire and Angels' is read as if it were
prose, it becomes more difficult than it needs to be. At the end of the
first stanza, Donne resolves the question by making a statement which
although it is not strictly logical, makes emotional sense: "I did love
aske, and now/ That it assume thy body, I allow,/ And fixe it self in
thy lip, eye, and brow."

Since his soul must love Ann through her body (there is no other
way), he asks love – i.e. his sense of what was missing before when
he was making love to various women's parts – to 'assume' a body
(this is like the incarnation of Christ, God 'made flesh' so that humans
can see him) which turns out to be Ann's. So paradoxically, he can
now "allow" the essence of his love, which is also the essence of
Ann, to be made manifest in her parts: "lip, eye, and brow." Donne
has gone from rejecting the love of a woman for her parts – back to
the love of a woman through her parts. And he has achieved this by
an act of faith in his own vision: by asking love.

A prose paraphrase must add too many words. The poem itself
makes the point. However, it leaves Donne with a new dilemma:

Whilst thus to ballast love, I thought,
And so more steddily to have gone,
With wares which would sinke admiration,
I saw, I had love's pinnace overfraught,
Ev'ry thy haire for love to work upon
Is much too much, some fitter must be sought:

> For, nor in nothing, nor in things
> Extreme, and scatt'ring bright, can love inhere ...

As Patrides points out, Donne is not only overloading a small boat (a pinnace) with the weight of his love, he is making it into a whore ('pinnace' was Elizabethan slang for a prostitute, presumably because it sailed back and forth between vessels in harbour, trading in various wares), and of course he is overloading his penis (= "pinnace"). Why must his love become so weighty? Because now it has license – by the poet's act of faith – to pay attention to parts, it finds there are too many of them! Each hair, even, is a part which can be loved. Which is "much too much." It turns out that love cannot successfully "inhere" in nothing (no thing – a substanceless angel), or in things: the woman's parts, her hairs – which scatter brightly as does the light from an angel.

There is also the strong possibility of a pun on 'air' and 'hair'. Again, Elizabethan pronunciation, which like ours varied from place to place, cannot be definitively known. But until very recently, some speakers (and they still do in Ireland) pronounced words of Norman French origin without the aitch, e.g. 'herb' as 'erb', and 'humour' as 'umour'. Since 'hair' is an Anglo-Saxon word (cf. German 'Haar'), the aitch is more likely to be sounded. But Londoners do (and did in Donne's day) tend to drop their aitches ... There is a good chance that 'Aire and Angels' is also about (h)air and angels.

Back to the problem – and a new resolution:

> Then as an Angell, face and wings
> Of aire, not pure as it, yet pure doth weare,
>   So thy love may be my loves spheare;
>   Just such disparitie
> As it twixt Aire and Angells puritie,
> T'wixt womens love, and mens will ever bee.

In order to be seen, an Angel must put on an appearance made of air, "not pure as it, yet pure." Donne must settle for the fact that Ann is not literally an angel: she is not that pure, after all. (Her air is (h)air). Yet she is pure. And Donne's love is able to "inhere" (as he has said above with possibly, given Elizabethan pronunciation, yet another pun on hair: 'in-hair') in her by wearing her: she is a spheare around his love (and sexually around his penis), just as a spheare of air surrounds an angel.

Patrides' note asks perplexedly about the last three lines: "Do the lines assert that (1) women's love is purer than men's, (2) men's is purer than women's, (3) both, (4) neither?" Redpath would opt for (2): he states the lines mean "women's love is less pure than men's". Then, perhaps looking over his shoulder at his female department colleagues and anticipating the next faculty meeting, he adds that Donne is probably making a joke (in order, of course, to overturn the Petrarchan idea of woman as angel) which "I do not believe ... is to be read as an insult, or that it would have been taken as such by an intelligent woman."

All this misses the point. Donne has already described the "disparitie ... twixt Aire and Angells puritie", in the previous three lines. But he has now moved on a step to make a comparison which he announces grammatically with the simple words "as it". He says that "just such disparitie" as the one ("as it") between the purity of air and the purity of an angel, exists between women's love and men's love: he is not comparing the respective purities of women's love and men's love, he is noting the disparity itself. He is saying that there will always be a disparity between women's love and men's love, just as there is between air and angels: one is substantial (though invisible, except around an angel), one is not. He has described clearly in the poem his strategy to give substance to his love by making the "angel" whose presence he has always sensed, and whom now he has found as his Anngel, take on substance. In an angel this substance is air. In a woman it is flesh: like it or not, he must settle for her physical parts, down to the last hair on her head, and make love to her with his pinnace/penis as if she were like any whore. As noted, this is a somewhat blasphemous project, since his love (not him – he says, love) becoming flesh through her is like God's love becoming flesh through Jesus – and because in surrounding his love with the "spheare" of his woman, he is inside an angel. Clearly this strategy is his own – not Ann's. It is a man's project, not a woman's. By the end of the poem, he has achieved his goal: he has fulfilled his pure love through her flesh – her substance, which though "pure" is not "as pure" as an angel's. And what about Ann? What about her project? He knows nothing about it. So he stops – or, more accurately, the poem stops – when there is nothing more to be said beyond acknowledging the disparity.

That Donne's project was not, as critics like Stevie Smith would have us believe, the subjugation and phallic piercing, etc., of women, is clear from another well known poem, 'The Extasie'. Poor Donne. When he writes shatteringly honest poems about how difficult it is for him, a man, to become one with his beloved woman – through sex, which, after all, is something he can enjoy with many women, not only the one he loves – every admission of frustration or difficulty is seen as hostile to her. But when he writes serenely about a day spent so intensely close to his beloved that to all intents and purposes they are one – the poem is dismissed as "Platonic." (By Ezra Pound, of all people, among others). It begins:

> Where, like a pillow on a bed,
>   A Pregnant banke swel'd up, to rest
> The violets reclining head,
>   Sat we two, one anothers best;
> Our hands were firmly cimented
>   With a fast balme, which thence did spring,
> Our eye-beames twisted, and did thred
>   Our eyes, upon one double string …

This is seen as unreal, as mystical. What a fantastically forced image! – the eye-beames threading the eyes on a double string. But perhaps there is a bio-electrical field around the body that official science has not yet arrived at explaining, although fringe science discusses it. This 'aura', in which air becomes visible, is like the "spheare" which Donne described angels as taking on. Perhaps he saw a genuine light around Ann (and especially her (h)air), like the blue light which the 20th century Russian poet Alexander Blok described as around his beloved's head.

If the eye-beams are not taken literally, they can at least join the metaphors of the poem. The lovers are "cimented", "so to'entergraft" their hands:

> All day, the same our postures were,
>   And wee said nothing, all the day.

And, after further description of this mingling of souls:

> This Extasie doth unperplex
> (We said) and tell us what-we-love,
> Wee see by this, it was not sexe ...

The other straightforward use by Donne in his poems of this dread word 'sex' – again, as in 'The Primrose' in an assertion that what is being felt is not sex. So is this another poem to Magdalen Herbert, another version of 'Platonique Love'? But Donne must always be read word for word. Note the parenthesis: "(We said)". The ecstasy of being one for a whole day without moving seems to suggest (they say) that it is "not sexe". The poem goes on to describe, famously, how love "interinanimates two soules", but soon returns to the question:

> But O alas, so long, so farre
>   Our bodies why doe we forbeare?
> They are ours, though not wee, Wee are
> The intelligences, they the spheare.
> We owe them thankes, because they thus,
>   Did us, to us, at first convay,
> Yeelded their forces, sense to us,
>   Nor are drosse to us, but allay.

Here we are again, back with 'Aire and Angels': "Wee are/ the intelligences, they the spheare." Although the "extasie" – which means, in Greek, a "standing outside", that is of the self – is a one-ness of intelligences, Donne is saying this is only possible because the lovers have been together physically, they have experienced 'sex'. Their bodies, which they forbeare (deny) during the ecstatic experience of the day, "yeelded their forces, sense to us", and what is more, they are not "drosse to us, but allay": they are not to be rejected like the by-product of a chemical process, but accepted as "allay" – meaning 'alloy', the blending together of two metals to form a new metal. (In Donne's day, nothing was known of atoms and molecules: an alloy, for example bronze blended from copper and tin, was a new metal, a new 'element' in its own right). The poem ends:

To'our bodies turne wee then, that so
Weake men on love reveal'd may looke;
Loves mysteries in soules doe grow,
But yet the body is his booke.
And if some lover, such as wee,
Have heard this dialogue of one,
Let him still marke us, he shall see
Small change, when we'are to bodies gone.

Some platonic poem! Not only is Donne saying that having spent the day in ecstasy without going to their bodies, they will now do so – as they have done before, which is what makes this ecstasy of souls possible in the first place – but that any other lover who happens by, can learn from their example. Finally, in a typical turning upside down of Christian imagery, Donne says that the observer will notice "small change" when the lovers replace their spiritual ecstasy with a physical one. (Just as when a devout Christian dies there is "small change" as he or she replaces physical existence with a spiritual one).

In 'The Extasie' Donne resolves the problem left at the end of 'Aire and Angels': now there is no "disparitie" between women's love and men's love, or at least between Donne's love and Ann's love. Of course, there is no evidence that he wrote it after 'Aire and Angels', except the evidence of sense. But it is fairly clearly written to Ann. If to Magdalen Herbert, it would in fact be platonic – but it is anti-platonic. And it does pick up the theme of 'Aire and Angels' which, since it celebrates a culmination of true love with an 'anngel', after a series of false starts, was as certainly written to Ann as any of Donne's poems.

Even during the difficult years, at Pyrford and Mitcham, when Donne, having risked all and lost all for love, had to endure watching Ann bearing children in a poverty for which he felt responsible – to the point that he had to struggle with "desperation" (depression), and to stave off thoughts of suicide by writing a book, *Biathanatos* , about it – he seems to have preserved a loving tenderness towards her, which is evident in the many poems he wrote about various partings, not only the rather formal *Valedictions*, but the simple 'Song' which according to Walton he wrote for Ann before leaving on one of his (politically ambitious) voyages to Europe. (Walton thought this was in 1611, but as usual his dates are shaky: it may have been earlier, in 1605).

> Sweetest love, I do not goe
> For weariness of thee ...

If Ann needed reassurance, who can blame her under the circumstances? Voyages were so long, anything could happen, deaths could occur ... And Donne was writing 'platonic' verse letters (they really were platonic: they are not alive enough to be anything else) to the two Countesses. Perhaps her anxiety got on his nerves. According to Walton 'A Valediction forbidding mourning' was written on the same occasion as 'Sweetest love ...' (He had, earlier by the less deeply felt tone of the poem, already tried 'A Valediction of Weeping'). As usual Donne was capable of an extraordinary fusion of emotion and thought, not only in the much-admired conceit of the parting lovers as the two ends of a spreading geometric compass, but in the preceding images of a sheet of gold being beaten out thinner and thinner, and of a love "so much refin'd,/ That our selves know not what it is."

Given what we know about the difficulties of Donne's life, it is extraordinary that almost all of the poems thought to have been written to Ann are so positive. At least, where considering negative questions, he is fighting through to a positive resolution of them. And most of the poems are downright happy – a rarity in English or any poetry. Donne expressed his unhappiness not in poetry but in letters and prose of a formal nature, unconnected with his domestic life. Only occasionally a sour note about his domestic life creeps into a letter, as in his reference to his house as his "prison" (a word which connotated for him entrapment in the flesh), or into an essay. He was trying at one point to match his earlier *Paradoxes* with a series of *Problems,* though he wrote only half a dozen. *Number* II was 'Why hath the common opinion afforded woemen soules?' This reprise of a common question in medieval theology is not as unkind as it sounds. He concludes cynically that men do not want women to have souls, but have to admit them so that women, like men, can be drawn to the devil (who, Donne remarks, "does mischeefe" because he does not have a body, he is "all soule") and therefore to damnation. (As usual – in spite of his upbringing in the atmosphere of Catholic martyrdom, another subject he wrote about unfavourably in a pamphlet,

Pseudo-Martyr, which made an impression on James I – he shows a robust attachment to the body.) His main point about women is that men want to grant them souls to make them less powerful. But in describing this power he shows some irritation:

> Have they so many Advantages and meanes to hurt us (for even their loving destroys us) that wee dare not displease them, but give them what they will, and so, when some call them Angels, some Goddesses, and the Peputian Heretikes make them Bishopes, wee descend so much with the streame to allow them soules.

"Even their loving destroys us". This is perhaps a reference to the old-fashioned belief that every ejaculation takes a day (or a week, or whatever) off the life. But it goes further into a consequence of the very thing Donne had so happily found with Ann: constancy.

Again in prose, *Paradox* II, 'A Defence of Womens Inconstancy', which expounds in witty but doctrinal form the line he had taken in his rebellious early poems, he remarks:

> I would you had your Mistresses so constant that they would never change, no not so much as their Smockes, then you should see what a sluttish virtue constancy were.

He would never have found Ann sluttish (she very obviously was not), but he did in one poem, 'Loves Alchymie', discover a level of disgust which, even before the current wave of correctness, was found offensive, and even by historical-minded Oxford academics – "insulting" to women (Helen Gardner), "deliberately outrageous" (J.B. Leishmann). In some manuscripts an alternative title for this poem is given: 'Mummy':

> Some that have deeper digg'd loves Myne then I,
> Say, where his centrique happinesse doth lie:
>   I have lov'd, and got, and told,
> But shoulde I love, get, tell, till I were old,
> I should not finde that hidden mysterie
>   Oh, 'tis imposture all:
> And as no chymique yet th'Elixar got,
>   But glorifies his pregnant pot,
>   If by the way to him befall

Some odoriferous thing, or medicinall,
So, lovers dreame a rich and long delight,
But get a winter-seeming summers night.

Our ease, our thrift, our honor and our day,
Shall we, for this vaine Bubles shadow pay?
  Ends love in this, that my man,
Can be as happy'as I can; If he can
  Endure the short scene of a Bridegroomes play?
  That loving wretch that sweares,
  'Tis not the bodies marry, but the mindes,
  Which he in her Angelique findes,
  Would sweare as justly, that he heares,
In that dayes rude hoarse minstralsey, the spheares.
Hope not for minde in women; at their best
Sweetness and wit, they're but Mummy, possest.

This is a bitter self analysis in which Donne revisits images from his earlier poems and undoes them. The reference to digging "loves Myne" in order to find where "centrique happinesse" lies, is to 'The Sunne Rising', where "the'Indias of spice and Myne ... lie here with me". (The Myne of his woman's insides is also, being possessed, what is 'mine'). Donne has loved, "got" (meaning begotten children – and poems), and told (in poems). But even if this loving, getting and telling were to continue until he is old, he has now given up on finding the hidden mystery of where sexual ("centrique" always implies this in Donne's poems) happiness lies. He wonders if it has all been an imposture, a deception. (This is not an unusual thought for poets: Robert Graves in old age would fret about whether "it was all worth it").

Donne then revisits another earlier image, the one from 'The Comparison', of the truly loving man's "masculine equall fire" inspiring "cherishing heat" in his woman's "best lov'd part", as an alchemist does in his "Lymbecks warme wombe". Now, the "chymique" (love's alchemist, Donne himself), even if some minor event (a new smell, or a medicinal by-product) occurs in his unfulfilled search for the "elixar" which would produce gold, "glorifies his pregnant pot." From "warme wombe" to "pregnant pot": this seems to have been the progress of Ann. To call someone a 'pot' was then something like calling someone a 'bag' now.

In *Poets Through Their Letters,* the poet Martin Seymour-Smith points out that the "winter-seeming summers night" is a reference to "the brevity of the sexual act." But for the Donne of the early poems, the act was far from brief: he relishes prolonging it, and it is indeed "a rich and long delight". The point is that now it is brief. Why? Because, keeping within the terms of reference of the poem, Ann is pregnant.

Donne's "ease", his "thrift" (his money: prosperity), and his "honor" had all been lost (paid out) at the end of his day in the sun, as it were – his glittering career before the disaster of his secret marriage. Now, he feels, it was all for a "vaine Bubles shadow". On the first level this is the common trite image of life as a bubble. But in this context there are other levels. A bubble is pricked, after all. The pregnant Ann is swollen and rounded. But, since they are both tired and ageing, she is probably a 'shadow' of what she was: not only Donne's early love for her, but she herself, is seen as having been a vain bubble.

The next image also revisits the point of 'The Comparison' – that subtle point that the experience of love is transformed through true and gentle loving, and that harsh possession of the woman makes her into something ugly. But whereas in 'The Comparison' Donne confidently distanced himself from the gross experience of the other man, he now wonders if, after all, his loving is different from that of anyone else. His "man", meaning his servant (and himself, his "man", his penis), so long as he can go through the rough scene of a marriage ceremony and feast (one thinks of Breughel's picture of a country wedding), might claim as justly as Donne that "in that days rude hoarse minstralsey" – the crude music of a public wedding – he is hearing the music of the spheres. Donne's own wedding, private and loving, and the poems he has written to Ann, are after all no better than any other man's experience.

This question of whether the experience of love is in fact unique had long haunted Donne. (It may even explain why in 'The Curse' he is so keen that other men should not know "who is my Mistris": knowing her from his description might enable them to imagine making love to her, perhaps to possess her as thoroughly, in their minds, as Donne himself does.) Robert Graves took up the question in the 20th century:

> The parson to his pallid spouse,
> The hangman to his whore
> Do not both utter the same vows,
> Both knock on the same door?

Seymour-Smith provides a dense analysis of the last couplet of 'Mummy', which is worth seeking out. He reviews the literature about 'Mummy' – "the theory ... that dead bodies, preserved in bitumen, acted as a restorative" – and quotes from a letter Donne wrote on 14th March 1608 to his friend Goodyer:

> The later Physitians say, that our natural inborn preservative is corrupted or wasted, and must be restored by a like extracted from other bodies; the chief care is that the Mummy have in it no excelling quality, but an equally digested temper ...

If Donne had come across discussions of the substance 'Mummy' in his reading at this time, it seems likely that this provoked the imagery of his poem 'Mummy', by coming together with the fact of Ann's pregnancy. Their daughter Lucy was christened in August 1608, which confirms the fact that Ann was pregnant in March. She too was "Mummy".

Seymour-Smith's conclusion about the final couplet of the poem is:

> ... the description of "possest" women as mummies does not carry with it merely the attribution of "dead, good for nothing". It means (1) that they have been reduced to sexual objects by the exercise on them of pure lust, and (2) that they are used by men merely to relieve themselves sexually, in a wholly unserious, "medical" (therapeutic) manner: they are "preserved" by men for this very purpose.

This is surely a valid reading of what Donne is saying about the consequences of possession. But on the personal level, he is also taking stock of where he has arrived in his relation with Ann. The phrase "Hope not for mind in women" is (for once justifiably) seen as offensive. But it must surely be seen in the context of the poem which is not about "women" but about one woman. A few lines earlier Donne mocks his "man" (himself, his penis) for swearing in the excitement of a wedding feast that "'Tis not the bodies marry, but the mindes". But he immediately follows with "Which he in her Angelique findes". Although he is mocking his own idealism, he is acknowledging that he did find Ann's mind "angelique". This is clear from all his poems to her, and as previously discussed, there is ample evidence that of all the woman he knew (including the 'intellectual' ones) she was the most capable of causing him to think.

Now, however, he cannot hope for "minde" in her. (A pun: he is also advising men not to hope for their wives to become pregnant – a result of being 'mined'). Even the "sweetness and wit" he once could expect from her is no longer there. Why? Because she is pregnant. The point deserves underlining, because otherwise Donne's bitter remark about not hoping for mind in women will be taken, as it always apparently is, to mean he is talking about women in general, at all times. And not only is she pregnant, she is Mummy. She already has four children.

There is a delicate point to be made here. The most intelligent and independent-minded of women experience emotional turbulence and fluctuating concentration during such transforming processes as pregnancy and breast-feeding. (Ann Donne could quite likely have found herself breast-feeding one child while pregnant with another – a sacrifice of the self which some devoted mothers make, even today). It is not just a question of 'hormones', it is fatigue, preoccupation, discomfort ... These are not times either for intellectual exchanges as formerly, or for passionate lovemaking. A woman who is exhausted may well make herself available to her husband, and affectionately allow him to possess her. But she may not be so hot with initiatives as before. Surely men and women will have experienced something like this? It does not, however, bring out the best in men. Because men bring to women not only sexual desire for them, but some element of desire to be mothered. This is hardly healthy, and if men are not neurotic they swiftly grow out of this false expectation when children are born and men must realise that their wife is 'Mummy' to the children – not to men. Which is just as well, because if a man identifies his wife with his mother, his sexual desire will fade fast: we do not make love to our mothers.

Nevertheless, some infantile desire for wife to be 'Mummy' may rear its ugly head in men at times. And Donne must be given credit for facing this and its consequences, as he does in the last killer statement – not an attack on Ann, but on himself – that "women ...

are but Mummy, possess." In other words, he no longer desires Ann, because in his possession of her he has made her into a mother and he does not desire his mother.

'Mummy' is a remarkable poem, of great courage, in going closer to the bone about the relation between a man's feelings for his wife as woman, and his wife as mother, than most men dare – or than is achieved, for that matter, in the works of Freud.

Donne's desire for Anne obviously returned: they had more children, until finally she died after childbirth, less than ten years after 'Mummy', and he was left devastated: he could never bring himself to marry again. But writing such a poem may have added to his "desperation". It may also have contributed to his turning away from poetry – except when on a few later occasions it forced itself on him. (Most of the *Divine Poems*, even, had been written by this time).

One question remains: what about Ann? How did she feel about her married life? The *Valediction Poems* suggest that she wept and worried if Donne had to go far away. The Latin inscription Donne had carved on her tombstone portrays her as affectionate and devoted. But her death, in the cliché, "worn out from childbearing", leaves some doubt. She had borne nine children under more desperate circumstances than those she found herself in, bearing the tenth, in 1617. Is there a possibility that she was ready to give up, finally? Although Bald dismisses her as "a devout girl", there is no documentation of this. Was she really delighted at her Jack Donne eventually becoming ordained as the pious Doctor Donne?

5   Divine Poems

In the not wholly dark days at Pyrford and Mitcham, Donne was much occupied with theological reading, and Helen Gardner's impeccable edition has made it clear that almost all the *Divine Poems*, once thought to follow Donne's ordination, were written between 1603 and 1608.

Helen Gardner, in spite of her admiration of the *Divine Poems* and their "moral intensity", sees that they do not rise to the same level as the love poems:

> In his love poetry he is not concerned with what he ought or ought not to feel, but with the expression of feeling itself ... As a love poet he seems to owe nothing to what any other man in love had ever felt or said before him; his language is all his own. As a divine poet he cannot escape the language of the Bible, and of hymns and prayers, or remembering the words of Christian writers.

Helen Gardner remarks that compared to the love poems, the divine poems are "willed." This is most clear in the *Holy Sonnets* which include the seven sonnets of 'La Corona', and which are dedicated to none other than Magdalen Herbert. Here at last, in this relationship which continued through most of their lives, Donne seems to have found the level at which they could best communicate – not through sex, not even through the squib of Platonic love, but through "willed" and carefully thought out Christian devotions.

Donne seems to have spent much of his time between 1603 and 1608, when his worldly career had been blocked, thinking about 'the meaning of life'. This is a vulgar way to describe the process, but it may help explain how he inevitably came back, after his years of rebellion, to Christianity. Because given the state of the kind of knowledge we call science in Donne's time, contemplating the meaning of life had to lead to Christianity. It was the only explanatory scheme available to a critical mind like Donne's. This may seem paradoxical, given that modern textual and historical research on the Bible leaves its literal truth intact only for the most credulous and uncritical fundamentalists. But it can be seen from Donne's early prose works and from the 'Anniversaries', that he was a veteran of theological argument while despising it in and of itself, and that he found scientific argument no more convincing. For Donne there was no Big Bang theory, no Darwinian theory of evolution – and nothing even remotely as coherent. Rather there was a series of observations and conjectures, which succeeded each other according to controversy. The word 'science' was not used other than in the limited sense of a specialised knowledge: what we call science was still called 'philosophy'. Modern science may seem cold comfort as a successor to Christianity, but it does at least make more sense than 'philosophy' did in Donne's day – it provides a whole system. One day it will all collapse in the face of new facts: the universe will turn out to be made of green cheese, or to be only 5,000 years old after all, or unimaginable discoveries will be made ... then we shall have to make another system. Systems are abstract and ultimately sustained by faith or by will. Donne's torment about his Christianity had less to do with argument than with his own capacity for such faith or will. Theology was less important to him than the Passion. (As Platonic theorising about love was less important to him than his actual emotional and sexual life.) Furthermore, the alternative to Christianity would be atheism, which was an essentially frivolous doctrine, in which the world could only be seen as entirely meaningless – as flux. And Donne had worked through his celebration of flux – change for its own sake.

Whether Christian or not (and if statistics are to be trusted, most readers of this book, in the UK at least, are only nominally Christian), the reader of Donne's *Divine Poems* will only be moved when the poems are human, concrete, personal. If they are about the love of God, they succeed most when this love is most like a human love – or even a sexual one. This is true of other Christian poetry as well: it is the passion in the mystical poems of St Theresa, of Juana de Asbaje, or of Southwell which reaches us, and the human detail. Less known examples are the Old Irish poems in which St Ite rejoices in the fact that she has breasts with which to suckle Christ, or the boy Jesus is portrayed making sparrows out of mud, which then fly away.

By these standards, the *Sonnets* in 'La Corona' fail. They are too formulaic, and too abstract. For example, *Sonnet* 2, 'Annunciation':

> Salvation to all that will is nigh,
> That All, which alwayes is All every where,

Which cannot sinne, and yet all sinnes must beare,
Which cannot die, yet cannot chose but die.

Here we can also see that Donne has returned to formal rhetoric, of the kind he must have had drummed into him at Oxford and Cambridge. This rhetoric comes through in the wrangling of his love poems, but it bursts free because the love poems are open systems where the divine poems are closed systems. The *Divine Poems* spark less interest than the love poems, not only because of their subject, which is not of urgent interest to other than practising Christians, but because they present fewer intrinsic problems to be discussed. In the love poems, Donne is saying new things about a subject which both excites and worries most of us. And since the poems often stretch his own highly intelligent mind to the limit, we have to strain all our attention to follow him. There are vital difficulties to be resolved. But the difficulties in the *Divine Poems* are for the most part not intrinsic, they are extrinsic. The poems are written to a frame of reference, which includes the Bible, the techniques of meditation and of formal contemplation which Donne must have learned as a boy, and Renaissance theological controversies. Most difficulties which occur can be resolved not by a close and loving reading, such as the love poems demand, but by reference to the notes in a good scholarly edition, such as Helen Gardner's.

Most readers prefer the *Holy Sonnets*, 19 in all, which are given the heading of *Divine Meditations*. They are less abstract, and so become unforgettable. "At the round earth's imagin'd corners, blow/ your trumpets, Angells ...", "Batter my heart, three person'd God ..." "Death be not proud ..." "I am a little world made cunningly/ Of elements ..."

The lines stick because, while rhetorical, they are intimate, and detailed. The sonnets not only begin powerfully, as with the lines given above, they end powerfully. "These are my best dayes, when I shake with feare.", "... for I ... never shall be free,/ Nor ever chast, except you ravish me.", "And thou like Adamant draw mine iron heart."

The last line might be written in a love poem. Donne addresses God as intimately as he does Ann or his other loves: he talks to God, no holds barred, and bares his soul as freely as in *Elegy* XIX he bares his body to his love. "Full nakedness!"

In undertaking this intense monologue directed to God, Donne does not escape the same traps his extreme intelligence inevitably causes him to fall into in any poetry he writes from the heart. Although he is conforming to a system, language itself – inspiration, rather than Donne's will – sometimes takes over, as it does almost always (Gardner's point) in the love poems. This can, being true poetry, create unexpected results. An example is "Death be not proud ...", which ends famously:

> One short sleepe past, wee wake eternally,
> And death shall be no more; Death, thou shalt die.

This is usually taken to be a statement of the triumph of life over death. But death has the last word: "Death thou shalt die".

'Goodfriday, 1613. Riding Westward', now considered to have been written in 1610 (the title was added by someone other than Donne), stands out among the *Divine Poems* for its informal thoughtfulness. Even a reader unsympathetic to its devotional message can sympathise with Donne's very human wish to turn his mind on higher thoughts (in this case to the East, the scene of Christ's passion) while occupied with baser needs (for Donne, having to ride West on business):

> Pleasure or businesse, so, our Soules admit
> For their first mover, and are whirl'd by it.
> Hence is't, that I am carryed towards the West
> This day, when my Soules forme bends towards the East ...

If many or most of Donne's *Divine Poems* were in fact written during the early years of his marriage, the implications of this for their meaning are still not taken fully into account by critics, who still see them as if forming a separate group – as indeed they have done in all editions of Donne's poems. He may have wished it this way, in instructions to friends about posthumous publication, or in his abortive considerations of publishing them just before his ordination: it suited him to separate the profanely swiving Jack Donne from the piously preaching Doctor Donne. Even now, some pious readers of Donne expostulate on how the themes of the love poems – surrender and possession, body and soul – reappear in a higher form in the divine poems. But this contradicts both what we now know about the chronology, and the evidence of the poems themselves, which reveal no such separation between the sacred and the profane. Take the most famous of the *Holy Sonnets* XIV:

> Batter my heart, three person'd God; for, you
> As yet but knocke, breathe, shine, and seeke to mend;
> That I may rise, and stand, o'erthrow mee'and bend
> Your force, to breake, blowe, burn and make me new.
> I, like an usurpt towne, to'another due,
> Labour to'admit you, but Oh, to no end,
> Reason your viceroy in mee, mee should defend,
> But is captiv'd, and proves weake or untrue.
> Yet dearely'I love you,'and would be loved faine,
> But am betroth'd unto your enemie:
> Divorce mee,'untie, or breake that knot againe,
> Take mee to you, imprison mee, for I
> Except you'enthrall mee, never shall be free,
> Nor ever chast, except you ravish mee.

From a Christian point of view, this poem has rightly been seen as in the mystical tradition of seeking a union with God which parallels the sexual union of man and woman, and more abstractly that of Christ and His Church. (A similar abstractness caused *The Song of Solomon*, a Hebrew love song probably used in pagan fertility rites, to be co-opted into the Bible and glossed as emblematic of Christ's love for the Church.) Like St Theresa (or Saint Ite, of whom he would not have known), so Donne in his passion uses sexual imagery to let God in. Not only is he the besieged town, occupied by the Devil with whom his weak powers of reason collaborate, who asks God to batter his walls down. He is also pleading with God to, in effect, rape him. Strong stuff, but then this is the same Donne who wrote the *Elegies*. Naturally, he thinks in sexual terms, although in his despair he now turns the tables on himself: instead of ravishing women with his powerful masculinity, he realises he must for once be passive and surrender, like a woman, to God's battering ram/penis. If the image is distasteful (not only because Donne is adopting the role of a woman but because that role is so passive, and God is seen as a sort of embodiment of masculinity and patriarchy), it is quickly forgiven because of its religious intent.

So far so good. But in the excitement of finding such an energetic and passionate religious poem, a naively Christian view can miss some more literal points which become obvious if the reader steps back a little and reads the poem for what it says rather than for its piety.

In the Christian context, it is assumed that the line "But am betroth'd unto your enemie" must mean that Donne is engaged to the Devil – not literally, of course. But why would the word "betroth'd" function only on a metaphorical level here? Demonstrably, Donne's love poems make sense first at a literal level, then at various levels of metaphor. Why should this not be true of his *Divine Poems*? To whom was Donne "betroth'd"? Not to the Devil (unless he was actively involved in witchcraft, which he was not), but to Ann. (It may be objected that he was not betrothed to her, but married to her – and in the next line he asks for a divorce – but strictly speaking a betrothal is not ended by marriage but continued by it.) At the first, literal level of this poem, it is Ann – not the Devil – who is God's "enemie".

Furthermore, in the next line, Donne bluntly asks God to "Divorce mee, 'untie, or breake that knot againe". He is, as he says earlier, "to 'another due", that is to another wife – Ann. She has "usurpt" him, i.e. taken him over. And he cannot escape from her. The only way out of the "prison" (as his letters describe it) of his marriage, is for God to release him – and then lock him up in a new prison. Only if he is imprisoned by God, and is God's slave ("enthrall me") instead of his wife's can he be free. Nor – he spells this out clearly – can he ever be chaste. Of course not: his prison with Ann is a sexual one. (Think of 'Mummy'.) And although the metaphor of his becoming a sort of bride of Christ is no doubt valid at the conventional Christian level, it takes on a new twist if the poem is read literally: Donne is saying that the only way he could possibly become free of his enthralment by Ann through sex would be if God made him into a woman. Then all future relationships would be with God, not Ann.

The poem is an extraordinary statement of Ann's power over Donne. And this may not only be a sexual power, but an intellectual one: "Reason ... is captiv'd." "Devout girl" though Bald assumes Ann to have been, she is God's enemy. And if, as seems likely, she had a mind of her own (not the same as being intellectually sophisticated – as Donne surely knew), the implication is that this mind was not so oriented to Christianity as Donne's was at the time.

Finally, Ann (or if the above biographical interpretation is rejected, some more general power of sex) wins at the end of the poem: Donne is not a woman, he is not yet ravished, and he is still betrothed to God's enemy.

It was only after Ann's death in 1617 that Donne was truly "free" to become a great Divine: his ordination in 1615, as even Bald admits, was in many ways a cynical exercise. The *Divine Poems* may represent more wishful thinking than is generally assumed, although this is broken through by the savage honesty of true poetry, which often subverts Donne's intended message.

6   From Poetry to Prose

Every poet, being human, lives a prose life, thinks prose thoughts, writes prose letters. Poetic life and thinking occur only at rare moments. But so long as these moments occur not too infrequently, poetry tends to take priority. A letter, or even a book of prose if the poet is more generally a writer, are not felt to be as important as a poem. And poetic thinking influences the prose. But sometimes, as with Donne, poetry either dies out or becomes progressively impossible, and prose takes over. In Donne's long set piece poems – 'Verse Letters to Severall Personages' (which he referred to in a letter as "the sallads and onions of Micham"), 'The Progresse of the Soule', and the 'Anniversaries' – prose thinking influences the poetry. By the time, when aged from 45 to his death at 59, he was capable of the sustained prose rhetoric of his sermons (about 160 of them eventually published, at about 8,000 words each), he had put poetry behind him and was writing hardly any. Conversely, when we know him to have been writing most poetry, from his late teens until age 35 or so, his prose writing was confined to letters and to brief essays such as the *Paradoxes* (from the early 1590s), the *Problems* (probably from the early 1600s) and the remarkable *Biathanatos*.

Biathanatos. A Declaration of that Paradoxe, or Thesis, that Selfe-homicide is not so Naturally Sinne, that it may never be otherwise was published in an edition as visually elaborate as its title is verbally elaborate, in 1647, years after Donne's death. He had left it with a friend saying that it should not be published since it was "misinterpretable", but not also destroyed. It is thought to have been written in 1608, the same year as 'Mummy'.

It is not a difficult read, although to the modern mind it is over-weighty with allusions, and it is constructed along neo-classical lines, like most Elizabethan prose, so that it starts boldly then seems to tail off after digressions in all directions. (We now tend to expect expository prose to save its punch lines for the end). The beginning is indeed striking:

> Beza [a leading French Calvinist theologian] … confesseth
> of himself, that only for the anguish of a Scurffe, which

over-ranne his head, he had once drown'd himselfe from the
Millers bridge in Paris , if his Uncle by chance had not then
come that way; I have often such a sickly inclination,

The word "Biathanatos" is Donne's own Greek coinage, and
means something like 'death of life'. Donne does not use the word
'suicide', but always 'self-homicide'. His argument is made in three
parts.

First, he argues that self-homicide is not necessarily due to
"desperation". (The word 'depression' had already appeared in
Elizabethan English in something like our sense, but was not further
developed until Burton's *Anatomy of Melancholy,* 1621.) Donne's
view of desperation is strict: it is a "sinne ... springing from Sloth
and Pusillanimity". He remarks, "I have the keys to my prison in
mine own hand, and no remedy presents itselfe so soone to my heart,
as mine own sword." But he does not believe self-homicide on
account of this sin is justifiable. He has more sympathy for the
individual and collective self-homicide of some of the early martyrs
in their eager welcome of death, and even for the "sickly inclination"
such as Beza's.

Second, he argues that laws against self-homicide are justifiable,
even though they often seem absurd, as when it is "the custome of
all Nations now to manacle and disarme condemned men, out of a
sore assurance that else they would escape death by death."

Third, he argues, unexpectedly, that Christ committed self-homicide: "this actuall emission of his soule, which is death, and which
was his own act, and before his naturall time". This was, however,
part of God's plan: just as he decided to take on the flesh so as to be
visible to men (back to 'Aire and Angels'), so he decided to die and,
as it were, rid himself of the flesh.

The arguments tail off at the end of the treatise. But Donne makes
a clear statement of his own position:

> I abstained purposely from extending this discourse to
> particular rules or instances ... because I dare not professe
> my self a Maister in so serious a science.

This statement is another one which might well be hung up on a
wall – in this case of the rooms where clinical discussions, psycho-

logical postmortems as it were, are held about why someone has committed suicide. The discussions can rage furiously, especially where the psychiatrist or psychologist has been drawn in to feeling responsible for not getting a patient out of depression ("desperation"), and the question of whether 'rational suicide' can exist produces heated exchanges. It shouldn't. According to the 1994 *Health of the Nation* document, two thirds of suicides in the UK are by people who have never been seen for a mental health problem. This supports Donne's assertion that self-homicide is not necessarily due to "desperation": it can be due to all manner of impulses and reasons.

Donne's wise *Biathanatos* should be better known. But it is probably still "misinterpretable". It is certainly evidence of Donne's extraordinary originality of mind. How could a person like this possibly – in the early 17th century or now – earn a living by remaining honest?

Donne's next prose work, *Ignatius his Conclave,* was written in 1610, published in 1611. Since it is an anti-Jesuit tract, and became part of Donne's armamentarium in his efforts to obtain preferment from James I, it is often viewed distastefully. (It is omitted from the otherwise excellent Penguin book *John Donne. Selected Prose,* edited by N. Rhodes.) But it provides a tour of Donne's mind at a critical point between poetry and the Church, and in the nature of its imagination it anticipates the satirical prose of that other great poet who became a Dean, Jonathan Swift. (Swift, of course, may have read *Ignatius,* but there is also an affinity.)

Apart from an over-long speech by the work's anti-hero, Ignatius, which the narrator himself affects to find boring, *Ignatius* is still readable. It takes the form of a voyage to Hell by the narrator, who "in an Exstasie" (i.e. a standing outside the self, as in the poem 'The Extasie') finds that his soul has "liberty to wander through all places".

In Hell, the narrator discovers Lucifer holding court but having to deal cantankerously with a possibly even greater devil, Ignatius, the founder of the Jesuits, who wants not only to rule Hell along with Lucifer, but to control who shall be admitted. A series of figures appear and demand admission, among them Machiavelli, Paracelsus, and Columbus. What they have in common is that they are "Innovators": Machiavelli in the techniques of politics, Paracelsus as an anatomist and dissectionist who neglects the human whole for the parts, Columbus as a discoverer of new worlds, mathematicians for having "pretended that they had squared the circle", "those who had but invented new attire for women", and multitudes of theologians.

A superficial reading might make this seem like an apology for a know-nothing conservatism, and perhaps it was received as such by James I. But Donne, speaking ironically through the mouth of the cynical Ignatius, is quite aware that the Reformation which the Jesuits were founded to smash, and to which he himself adheres, was itself an innovation. As Ignatius puts it, "the ancient Religion was so much worne out, that to reduce it to the former dignity, and so to renew it, was a kinde of Innovation", to which Elizabeth I, whom Ignatius calls "the Lunatique Queen" was susceptible.

The innovation which Donne objects to is not renewal of thinking, or medical or physical discovery, but innovation for its own sake: the replacement of one established truth (or at a trivial level, a fashion) by another without any proper weighing of the evidence, and without moral consideration. For example, theologians have "induced doubts and anxieties, and scruples, and after, a libertie of beleeving what they would; at length established opinions, directly contrary to all established before." Donne's objection is in the same common-sense English literary tradition as later on Swift's to Lilliputians fighting wars over whether boiled eggs should be opened at the broad or the narrow end, and Lewis Carroll's to Humpty Dumpty claiming that "a word means what I say it means."

The irony of the tract is doubled by the fact that Ignatius himself wants to keep most of the Innovators out of Hell, where they would presumably question his authority, and Lucifer wants to let them in. There is a hint that, on this issue at least, Donne may be on the side of Lucifer, who is presented as somewhat harassed by the superior evil of Ignatius: although Donne attacks innovation for its own sake, he can see that it at least has the function of questioning the power-mad (as he sees it) authority of such as the Jesuits.

Lucifer's proposed solution is to make Galileo (who had started to map the surface of the moon through telescopic observations, and had discovered the moons of Jupiter) throw out a rope to the moon and pull it close to the Earth so that Ignatius can open a new Church which can "reconcile the Lunatique Church to the Romane Church ...", and "there will soone grow naturally a Hell in that world also". Then further Hells can be established in other "habitable starres". (This satire is still close to the bone in the 21st century: who is to say that if we colonise other worlds we will not establish in them our own Church of hellish shopping centres?)

Donne only lets his irony slip once in *Ignatius*, when he has Ignatius aver, having made much of the idea that the Moon must have a "lunatique" Queen, namely Elizabeth I: "Nor can I call to minde any woman, which either deceived our hope or scoped our cunning [i.e. foiled Ignatius' plans], but Elizabeth of England." And since James I was notoriously touchy about his obvious inferiority as a monarch compared with Elizabeth, it cannot be assumed that Donne was playing politics here. Elizabeth seems to have been much on his mind at this time.

Rather as the gloss "John Donne, Ann Donne, Undone" reflects a pivotal moment in Donne's worldly life, the 'Anniversaries', especially the first one which was initially called 'An Anatomie of the World', reflect a pivotal moment in the shift in his thinking from poetry to prose. The 'Anniversaries' were planned to commemorate, in verses every year, the death of a young girl, Elizabeth Drury, who died at the age of 14, in 1610. Donne had never met her, although he later became friends with her parents. To plan a project in this way is in itself characteristic of prose, not poetry. A previous effort at an ambitiously-planned poem, 'The Progresse of the Soule', had been started in 1601: it proposed to follow the transmigrations (satirically: Donne did not believe in reincarnation) of the soul of Eve's apple through various evil personages until it emerged in Donne's own day. (It has been thought, on no evidence, that the chosen vehicle of this soul was to have been Elizabeth I. But *Ignatius* makes it clear that Donne's regard for Elizabeth was high.) The 'Progresse of the Soule', after much strained mock-heroic rhetoric, fizzled out.

The project of the 'Anniversaries' also failed, in part because Donne's friends, including Jonson, thought it ridiculous, and he eventually seems to have shared their opinion and discontinued the series, as it were, after two episodes. The 'Anniversaries' contain what seem to be competing strands of thought: the scientific, the Christian, and the poetic. The verse is largely rhetoric, but there are disconcerting spasms of real poetry in which thought and emotion combine equally. One of these is a famous passage in which Donne expresses his own mental predicament and that of his age:

> And New Philosophy calls all in doubt,
> The Element of fire is quite put out;
> The Sun is lost, and th'earth, and no man's wit
> Can well direct him where to look for it.
> And freely men confesse that this world's spent,
> When in the Planets, and the Firmament
> They seeke so many new; they see that this
> Is crumbled out againe to his Atomies.
> 'Tis all in peeces, all cohaerence gone;
> All just supply, and all Relation:
> Prince, Subject, Father, Sonne, are things forgot,
> For every man alone thinkes he hath got
> To be a Phoenix, and that there can bee
> None of that kinde, of which he is, but hee.

Donne has often been called, in the 20th century, 'modern'. Perhaps this is because he takes nothing for granted and – at least until his ordination – manages to contain many strands of contemporary thought without making a final choice among them: he rejects certainty, while lamenting its absence. His life straddles the turn of the 16th and 17th centuries, a time when the intense conflict between Catholicism and Protestantism was at fever pitch. He contained this conflict within himself, as a Roman Catholic who became an Anglican. But he also read voraciously in 'philosophy', meaning science. There is evidence that he had read the *Somnium* by the astrologer/astronomer Johannes Kepler, which he must have seen in manuscript since it was not published during his lifetime. (Kepler himself, when he read the Latin version of *Ignatius his Conclave,* noted that Donne had obviously been reading his work). Bald concludes that Donne had access to such manuscripts through his visits to Ralegh and the Wizard Earl. Kepler's was the "philosophy" which "put out" fire, i.e. the idea that there was a *sphere* of fire in the heavens – thus destroying the classical and medieval theory of the four elements – by proving the absence of refraction of stellar light.

Another astrologer, Jerome Cardanus, who was no scientist and more a philosopher in the usual sense, had also put fire out by stating that it could not exist as an element because it was incapable of producing living creatures. Donne refers to this argument from Cardanus' *De Subtilitate* in one of his *Sermons* No. VII, and he must have known Cardanus' *Comfort,* which in its translation by Bedingfield was a huge but often unacknowledged influence on Elizabethan thinking. (Not least on Shakespeare's: Hamlet's "To be or not to be" soliloquy owes much to Cardanus, and it has been speculated that the book Hamlet is said to be reading in the play is *Comfort).* Donne would not, however, have agreed with Cardanus' belief that, in Bedingfield's translation, "Man is nothyng but his mynd." In fact, at the end of the passage quoted above, he rejects the idea that man can be a Phoenix – he agrees with Cardanus that no creature can be born from fire – but at the same time rejects the idea that man can stand alone, independent of matter. (As well, he could almost be lamenting the late 20th century 'Me generation'.)

It seems 'modern' in Donne that he envisions a universe in which all certainties are collapsing under the onslaught of science. He attempts to 'anatomise', i.e. dissect, the material world, as it crumbles under his hands, as it were, into "atomies". There is no more structure. It is characteristic of Donne, in his poems and in his prose preceding his ordination, that he never takes the easy way out. There were plenty of Elizabethan enthusiasts, like the Wizard Earl, for new ideas. Donne could have jumped, as others did, out of the Medieval mental world into the Renaissance one. But although he was up to date with science at what we would now call its cutting edge (not everyone had access to Kepler's manuscripts), he could not wholly accept it. In *Ignatius,* Donne mocks Kepler's claim that "no new thing should be done in heaven without his knowledge." Yet astronomers, like all 'innovators', end up contradicting each other, and their findings constantly change. Donne is putting his finger, early in the history of science, on a weakness that bedevils it still: that its demonstrable certainties keep changing. This was indeed the opposite of the Aristotelian fixed world adopted by the Church. But of course there were theological innovators too. His despair, in *Ignatius* and the 'Anniversaries' is that having destroyed the fixed medieval world, theological and scientific speculation have been unable to provide a satisfactory new one. The despair can only be overcome by an act of faith – which, in the 'Anniversaries', he devotes to Elizabeth Drury. He realises in the first 'Anniversary' that his (and science's) anatomy of the world is of dead structure: it excludes life. His metaphor for this is Elizabeth Drury's death. The world is dead – because she, who animated it, is dead.

This metaphor has been seen as a mere conceit, and under criticism from Ben Jonson, Donne admitted that he was only writing about "The Idea of a Woman". But this may have been merely a sop to Jonson. Neo-Platonism had been in fashion among Elizabethan sonneteers, such as Samuel Daniel who wrote a sequence to an imaginary woman whom he named "Idea." This is the ultimate extension of the tradition begun in Dante's *Vita Nuova* of sonnets to an idealised Beatrice and of Petrarch's sonnets to Laura. Donne could not write sonnets of this type: his love poems spring out of real, physical relations and choose their own varied forms. Only his *Holy Sonnets* were written as a deliberate sequence. Many of them, like many passages in the 'Anniversaries', seem written less from an act of faith than from an act of will, and consequently they fail as poetry.

It is worth emphasising, too, the word "a" in "The Idea of a woman." Not 'The Idea of Woman', as a generalisation or a Platonic form. Donne's neo-Platonism, such as it was, was only one contradictory element in a much more robustly physical approach to knowledge. Even after his ordination he could not be content with the idea that the soul was the only reality, the body mere dross: he sought, tormentedly, to demonstrate from the scriptures that in spite of the earthly body's rot, there would be a bodily resurrection. Before his ordination, he pursued a temperamental affinity for the hard facts of the new science ("new philosophy"). But just as he was unable to take the sort of neo-Platonic view which Cardanus had expressed, that man was nothing but his mind, he was also incapable of believing that man was nothing but his body. This latter view, which 20th century science glibly accepts, was a risky one in the early 17th, when to profess atheism (as Ralegh and the Wizard Earl were falsely reputed to do) was still a crime. Nevertheless it was implicit in the "new philosophy", and the stage was set for a century in which a scientist like Newton could split his mind in two and pursue physics on the one hand in purely material terms, and on the other profess Christianity, and in which the ultimate in philosophy was Descartes' rationalisation of such a split: "I think, therefore I am", but my body is a mere machine. It was another century again before La Mettrie had the daring to suppose (in *L'homme machine)* that since man's body was a machine, his mind was merely part of it – something

20th century scientists believe without question, even as they seek reason for being, in equating the Big Bang with God.

Donne was unable, being caught in his own time, to resolve the mind/body question in the dubious ways which were to follow. Once ordained, he resolved it through his act of faith/will. Before his ordination, it seems to have remained unresolved in his everyday mind and it clearly tormented him in his poems – which, in their own way (as in 'Aire and Angels') do resolve it. But it is not always possible to transfer the resolution in a poem into the language of the everyday mind – unless by thinking in poems. The mind has to invent a framework in which the truth of poems can exist. Perhaps as part of this, Donne grasped at what seems almost a pre-Christian act of particularistic faith in a woman:

> This is the worlds condition now, and now
> She that should all parts to reunion bow,
> She that had all Magnetique force alone,
> To draw, and fasten sundered parts in one;
> She whom wise nature had invented then
> When she observ'd that every sort of men
> Did in their voyage in this worlds Sea stray,
> And needed a new compasse for their way ...
> Shee, shee is dead; she's dead: when thou knowst this,
> Thou knowst how lame a cripple this world is.
> And learn'st thus much by our Anatomy,
> That this worlds generall sicknesse doth not lie
> In any humour, or one certain part;
> But as thou sawest it rotten at the heart ...

Donne's capacity not only to understand the new philosophy but to bring it alive in language shows here in the use of the word "magnetique" in both its current senses, the literally scientific one and the metaphorical of attraction – the first recorded use of the adjective in English. (A commentator, Coffin, has deduced that Donne is referring to William Gilbert's *De Magnete,* in which the earth was described as a magnet exerting a power of "coition".) "Reunion" is also the first use in English of this word which Donne would make much of in his sermons proclaiming the reunion of soul and body at the resurrection. A poem Donne may have read in manuscript was Ralegh's 'Epistle of the Ocean to Cynthia', where the thinking is similar: Ralegh's world is animated and inspired by 'Cynthia', Queen Elizabeth I, and when she is absent that world is dead. Donne's words above echo Ralegh's "Shee is Gonne, shee is lost! Shee is found, shee is ever faire!" And surely at one level the 'Anniversaries', about the death of the world following the death of a virgin called Elizabeth, are about the death of the world Donne was born into, when its great Virgin Queen, Elizabeth died.

There was a side of Donne – the poet in him – which would, it seems from the first 'Anniversary' and from the 'Nocturnall upon S. Lucies day', (not to speak of his many poems to Ann), have been content to worship a female principle as animating the world. Paradoxically, this very ancient belief can coexist with a sophisticated knowledge of science because it is rooted in the physical senses. Man (man or woman) is decidedly not, in this view, nothing but mind. It is not a Christian (or a Platonic) view. And it offers few consolations to thought, only a perpetual tension between the spiritual and the physical, with no clear idea which is which – any more than it is finally clear which is sex, which is love.

There was no support for such an all-encompassing view in the world in which Donne lived as the 17th century began, and his over-conscious attempt to make a compass out of Elizabeth Drury was bound to fail. It was a century in which people were forced to take sides – in England literally, later in the Civil War. Donne's way as a poet was to attempt to live all sides at once. But this must have worked no better in his personal life than in his public one. In a sense the 'Anniversaries' are disloyal to Ann. Did he love her, his wife – or the "Idea of a woman" as personified in a virgin girl whom he had never met? In the first 'Anniversary', Donne himself is cracking under the strain and risks crumbling into "atomies". No wonder he turned, finally, to the Church.

Donne's *Sermons* are mainly known because of two famous passages: "No man is an Island ...", and "Ask not for whom the bell tolls. It tolls for thee ..." But the reader who trawls through the almost one million words of the *Sermons* looking for equally exciting passages will be largely disappointed. The effect of the *Sermons* is mainly, as it was intended to be, cumulative. In preaching them, Donne used many images of urgency – the bell tolling, the sand running out of an hourglass ("There is not a minute left to do it; not a minutes sand ...")

to provoke anxiety about repentance in time for death. By several accounts, although his voice was not strong, his delivery was dramatic, charismatic. He kept an hourglass on the edge of the pulpit, ostensibly to time his sermons, but as a general reminder of time running out. His method was often in the seemingly immortal sermon tradition of first frightening his audience with images of death, then promising them rewards in heaven if they repented.

There are also frequent nasty references to the seductiveness of women, which no doubt fended off his own sexual desires now that he was a widower and resolved to live unmarried, but which coming from the same man who wrote the love poems seem shallow and hypocritical. In a *Sermon* from 1620, preached at Lincoln's Inn no less, scene of his youthful frolics, he took the text from Job, 'Corruption in the skin', dwelling on the fulminations of various classical authors, such as Tertullian: "there's vain-glory in their excess of clothes, but ... there's prostitution in drawing the eye to the skin"; and Pliny: "it was but an invention that women might go naked in clothes, for their skins might be seen through those clothes, those thinne stuffes." To which Donne adds his own observation that "Our women are not so carefull, but they expose their nakednesse professedly, and paint it, to cast birdlime for the passengers eye." He ends his peroration with the famous passage: "Between that excremental jelly which thy body is made of at first, and that jelly which thy body dissolves to at last; there is not so noysome, so putrid a thing in nature."

Although Donne's *Sermons* rest on a new certainty and, at least rhetorically, answer any questions which are posed in them, perhaps what makes parts of them most alive still is a sense of wonder and questioning about nature. Donne's knowledge of science was not wasted. The following passage might stand as a warning to the reductionist brain scientists of today, while at the same time respecting their science:

> We know the receipt, the capacity of the ventricle, the stomach of man, how much it can hold; and wee know the receipt of all the receptacles of blood, how much blood the body can have; so wee doe of all the other conduits and cisterns of the body; But this infinite Hive of honey, this insatiable whirlpoole of the covetous mind, no Anatomy, no dissection hath discovered

to us. When I look into the larders, and cellars, and vaults, into the vessels of our body for drink, for blood, for urine, they are pottles, and gallons; when I look into the furnaces of our spirits, the ventricles of the heart and of the braine, they are not thimbles; for spirituall things, the things of the next world, we have no roome; for temporall things, the things of this world we have no bounds.

In his *Sermons*, Donne was able through his powerful prose rhetoric to remain in control, and to state only unequivocal belief. Even here, though, he returned time and again to the question that had tormented him in his poetry and at times been resolved at a poetic level which, however, could not be integrated into the prose life of his day. What is the relation between body and soul? Now, he could settle the question, through dogma. Even though the body, which in his time he had loved so deeply, was now to be considered "noysome" and "putrid", it would be made loveable again in its "reunion" with the soul at the resurrection. (There is at least a back-hand acknowledgement in his frequent use of the word "reunion", that there was once a "union", such as he achieved in his poems.) His last great sermon, known as 'Deaths Duell', was said to be "The Doctors owne funerall sermon." It concludes:

Unto God the Lord belong the issues of death, and by the reanimating this dust into the same body, and reanimating the same body with the same soule, bee shall in a blessed and glorious resurrection give me such an issue from this death, as shall never passe into any other death, but establish me into a life that shall last as long as the Lord of Life himself.

In a conversation reported by Walton, which Donne is supposed to have had with a visitor on the day after he had preached 'Death's Duell', he said, "I now plainly see it was His [God's] hand that prevented me from all temporall employment; and that it was his Will I should never settle nor thrive till I entered into the Ministry." He even had the bad taste (or his visitor had, in his too accurate verbatim report of the conversation) to conclude that God "hath given me even at this present time some testimonies by his Holy Spirit, that I am of the number of his Elect ..." But the experience of writing inspired poetry will have made him feel, long before he turned to the

Church of England, that he belonged to another, more modest Elect – that of poets who, at least for a time, have a sense of truth and certainty. When he turned to the church, Donne brought his poetic conviction with him, and transferred it to the new certainties which he iterated in his sermons. Perhaps he would have been content with the word order under the statue of him, in his shroud, the face taken from a lifemask, (which survived the fire which destroyed his St Paul's and most of the City in which he grew up), and still stands there with the inscription: PREACHER AND POET. But he was nevertheless, as Ben Jonson knew, first a poet.

Nor had poetry utterly deserted him, in spite of his will to reject it. Which of Donne's poems was the last is unknown. For a while it was thought to be the 'Hymne to God the Father', in which Donne jokes familiarly with God, "But sweare by thy selfe, that at my death thy sonne/ Shall shine as he shines now ..." Rather as if God were to say, "By God!, I'll do it." (As Robert Frost put it: "Please, God, forgive my little jokes on Thee,/ And I'll forgive thy great big one on me.") But then it was pointed out that not only was Donne punning on his own name in the poem, he was probably also punning on Ann's name (More) in the refrain, "For I have More." The poem must have been written during his marriage.

One of the *Holy Sonnets* begins, "Since she whome I loved, hath payd her last debt/ To Nature and to hers ...", and was obviously written after Ann's death. This is an odd statement in a devotional poem, in which Ann's death might be described in Christian terms, for example as her being gathered up by God. Instead it could be a pagan statement: Ann has apparently borrowed from Nature what (life? beauty?) she must now repay. Since she died in childbirth, there is a hint that this was Nature (not God) gathering in her own. The "and to hers" implies that she paid, through death in childbirth, for having had a family. But why is this a debt? Children are usually considered to owe something to their mothers, not the other way round. Is Donne hinting that through her death she finally paid for her bad behaviour to her original family, in having run off with him? In the passage recorded by Walton's informant, when Donne concluded he was among the Elect, he also is quoted as thanking God for having permitted him to live "to be useful and comfortable to my good Father-in-law Sir George More, whose patience God hath been pleased to exercise with many temporal Crosses ..." It is hard to believe that the real John Donne, rather than the fantasy of a pious admirer, could arrive at such a degree of unctuousness. Unfortunately, as has already been noted, there are several such hints that Donne's return to practising Christianity after his years of painful freedom as a poet, his ordination, and his subsequent career as a Divine, involved a certain betrayal of his love for Ann.

But fortunately there is the great 'Nocturnall upon S. Lucies Day' which most commentators – even though they show little interest in Ann, and many have made unsuccessful efforts to show that the poem was written about Lucy, Countess of Bedford – agree to have been written in Donne's despair after Ann's death. It is her elegy in the original sense of the word – a poem of mourning. It has already been discussed briefly in the Introduction. Like 'The Primrose', at one level it too can be seen as a profoundly pagan poem, an invocation – although through the name of a Christian Saint, Lucy, or Light – to the ancient sun Goddess who brings life back to the dark earth on the shortest day of the year. When he wrote "let me prepare towards her" perhaps Donne was acknowledging a more ancient force than God the Father.

It is most likely, however, that his last poem was the 'Hymne to my God, in my sicknesse' in which as he prepares himself calmly for his death and resurrection, he notes in a detached and satisfyingly macabre way how:

> ... my Physitians by their love are growne
> Cosmographers, and I their Mapp, who lie
> Flat on this bed ...

An image which recalls the excitement of 'The Sunne Rising', when he and his beloved were not a flattened out map of the world, but the world itself:

> ... since thy duties bee
> To warme the world, that's done in warming us.
> Shine here to us, and thou art every where;
> This bed thy center is, these walls, thy spheare.

7   Reputation

He esteemeth John Done the first poet in the World in some
things ... affirmeth Done to have written all his best poems err
he was 25 years old ... now since he was made Doctor repenteth
highlie and seeketh to destroy all his poems ... Done for not
keeping of accent deserved hanging ... Done himself for not
being understood would perish.

In probably the earliest series of literary interviews – Drummond of
Hawthornden's *Conversations,* which took place in 1618 – the poet
and dramatist Ben Jonson provided the expected pithy remarks about
various contemporaries, but returned most often to his friend John
Donne. He also discussed specific poems – not the early short poems,
but the long ones Donne had written to influential patrons and
patronesses – mocking the far-fetched transmigrations in 'The
Progresse of the Soule', and saying that when he had remonstrated
with Donne that the subject of the 'Anniversaries' was not true to
life, Donne had said that he "described the Idea of a Woman, and not
as she was."

Drummond was the prototypical interviewer in making sure to
cut his subject down to size: "He is a great lover and praiser of himself,
a contemner and scorner of others, given rather to lose a friend than
a jest, jealous of every word and action of those about him (especially
after drink ...)" Jonson is portrayed in *Conversations* as a buffoon,
although no one would remember Drummond without him. His
remarks are often quoted, for their colourfulness (some critics might
well want to hang poets, but they do not say so), but seldom closely
examined. Yet only two years before, he had written the brilliant *The
Devil is an Ass,* and he had several more plays in him – and poems
too. He knew poetry, and he knew Donne – who may have been "the
first poet in the World in some things", but after a phase of writing
fake poetry for patrons who had not come across with their favours,
seemed to have sold out to a career in the church. In Jonson's eyes
he probably deserved hanging for much more than "not keeping of
accent".

Jonson, like Donne, was a strong Latinist. "Accent", by which
Jonson meant 'stress', not as is commonly assumed 'metre', is the

equivalent in English of quantity (an agreed system of vowel lengths) in Latin verse. Jonson's own verse, like that of most Elizabethans (the exceptions being the early Donne and the late Shakespeare), follows a sort of national agenda, set out in the many metrical treatises of the time, for English poets to write as the Romans had done, in a variety of brilliant set forms, though in their native 'accent'. The result was often a vacuous musicality, as in Lodge's:

> My bonny lass, throe eye,
>> So sly,
> Hath made me sorrow so.
> Thy crimson cheeks my dear
>> So clear,
> Have so much wrought my woe.

But when the writer had a true ear and sense, the result could be both poetry and music (not musicality), as in Jonson's own:

> Have you seen but a bright lily grow,
>> Before rude hands have touched it,
> Have you marked but the fall of the snow
>> Before the soil hath smutched it?
> Have you felt the wool o' the beaver?
>> Or swansdown, ever?
> Or have smelt o' the bud of the briar?
>> Or the nard in the fire?
> Or have tasted the bag o' the bee?
>> O, so white! O, so soft! O, so sweet is she!

In contrast, Donne's *Elegy* XI begins:

> Not that in colour it was like thy haire,
> For Armelets of that thou maist let me weare:
> Nor that thy hand is oft embrac'd and lost,
> For so it had that good, which oft I mist …

For Jonson, such natural speech rhythms could be put into dramatic dialogue (of which he was a master: "I fart at thee!", his play *The Alchemist* famously begins), but not into poetry. Elizabethan poetic diction was not quite natural, although it was a paradigm of naturalness compared to what it became in a long decline towards increasing artificiality (except in the hands of a few cranks like Rochester, Swift, and Blake) over the following 300 years. By the mid 18th century, when Donne was considered at all, he had to be 'adapted'. His poem 'The Indifferent' begins:

> I can love both faire and browne,
> Her whom abundance melts, and her whom want betraies,
> Her who loves lonenesse best, and her who maskes and plaies,
> Her whom the country form'd, and whom the town ...

As re-written for *The Gentleman's Magazine* in 1734, this becomes the vomit-making:

> Let my *Fair One* only be
> *Female Sex,* and she's for me:
> I can love her, *Fair* or *Brown,*
> Of the *Country* or the *Town.*

It was not until 1808 or so, when Coleridge and his friend Lamb became enthusiasts for Donne, in a climate of anarchic romanticism, that his voice could be heard again for what it was – although only by a few: Coleridge and Lamb were avoided as great bores when they took up reading Donne aloud at parties. Coleridge himself eventually subsided into the new turgidity of romantic diction ("like a fly in a gluepot", as he had described Schiller's equivalent verse in German), but he was able to sort out the problem of Donne's 'accent'. In a humorous verse on the subject he began "With Donne, whose muse on dromedary trots", but concluded that Donne's verse was "Wit's forge and fire-blast, meaning's press and screw." Coleridge believed that "the body of poetry is Good Sense", and he was prepared to allow Donne's sense to force his verse into its own shape. Coleridge also believed that in great poetry there is "a continuous undercurrent of feeling". His solution – which can still be recommended – to the problem of Donne's accent, was to read the poems aloud, paying close attention to the stress put on words by "meaning's press and screw" and by the feeling in them. "To read Dryden, Pope &c., you need only count syllables; but to read Donne you must measure time, and discover the time of each word by the sense of passion."

During the rest of the 19th century, Donne sank mainly out of sight. An edition by Grosart which appeared in 1872 made little impact. The Victorians' poetic bible, Palgrave's *Golden Treasury*, contained only one (very bad) poem ascribed to him, which was not written by him at all.

Donne was only widely read when Herbert Grierson's great Oxford edition of the poems appeared in 1912. (This was rightly seen as pioneering, in England. But J.R. Lowell and C.E. Norton, with typical Harvard Bostonian nerve, had brought out an influential, though less scholarly edition, in America, in 1895). The early 20th century provided a brief space when Hopkins' "sprung rhythms", Eliot's polyglot conversations in verse, and the colloquialisms of the First World War poets such as Sassoon, wrenched English metre into new shapes (a brief space because it was so quickly succeeded by its disintegration into 'free verse', in effect chopped prose, from which a few traditionalist poets stood aside and defensively returned to melliflousness) and in which poets and critics were ready to hear Donne's poetry – in Grierson's words, "a poetry of talk, vigorous and direct."

But these cycles of poetic diction becoming congealed and formalised, then being renewed or revived in spasms of excitement, are the norm in poetry – in European languages, at any rate. Why did Donne's poetry not achieve a wide revival when Coleridge and Lamb were promoting it? Why did it have to wait another hundred years?

The answer may be in another of Ben Jonson's points, that "Donne himself for not being understood would perish." At first this is puzzling. Why should Jonson, of all people, find Donne hard to understand? As noted, both men were Latinists, who found their poetic roots in Juvenal, Martial, and Catullus – for Jonson, the dramatists such as Terence and Seneca as well – and they were close enough friends to be able to criticise each other's work bluntly: Jonson's objections to the 'Anniversaries' have been mentioned, and apparently a work was planned in the form of a dialogue in which Jonson would be called "Dramaticus", and Donne "Criticus". This was presumably abandoned, along with poetry, by Donne, which may explain some of Jonson's annoyance when talking to Drummond – duly turned into the judgment that he was a "contemner and scorner" of others.

Jonson was almost certainly not remarking that other people – not himself – found Donne hard to understand. He had enough natural poetic arrogance not to have cared a fig whether other people understood Donne or not, if he himself did. But his remark suggests, at least, that the legend of Donne's poetry being difficult had begun early. The source of this difficulty is usually said to be in Donne's 'conceits' – those extraordinary far-fetched images which in fact were common in earlier Elizabethan poetry. The word 'conceit' is derived from 'conceive', and it is much like a 'concept' in modern conceptual art: an idea is pushed to its limit, as when the Reichstag is wrapped in plastic, or whatever. But conceits do not have to be difficult. By almost a century after Donne they had deteriorated to the point where Dryden could write about a nobleman dying of smallpox and the pus from the pocks trickling down like tears of mourning. This is disgusting, but not difficult. Even Donne's famous conceit (versions of which were previously used by Omar Khayyám and by an Italian poet, Guarini, whom Donne may have read) of the two lovers, separating for a journey, being like the two halves of a geometric compass is, though extravagant, not difficult to follow. He pursued his conceits with an expert logic to especially paradoxical and ingenious conclusions, but in the early poems at least, they never detach themselves from reality in the way Dryden's revolting example does. It is not revolting because of its grossness, but because of its kitschness. The modern Czech writer Milan Kundera has defined kitsch as "the third tear", meaning that if the first reaction to an event is a tear, and the second is a self-conscious tear about the tear, kitsch is the self-indulgent tear about the tear about the tear ... Donne's worst efforts – his verse for his Countesses, his various 'Epicedes' and 'Obsequies', the second 'Anniversary' – occasionally reach this point of kitsch. But since they were written well after Jonson's cut-off point of Donne's decline after age 25, these were not the poems Jonson thought would "perish": they already had done so, in his eyes, if they had ever been alive at all. He was concerned – and it was a real concern, if Donne was indeed "the first Poet in some things" – about the early poems.

Donne's rigorously intellectual conceits were in fact a stimulation to his poetic successors, notably his disciples George and Edward Herbert, and later the brilliant Andrew Marvell. It was the squalid Dryden who gave them their main critical blow, in 1692, at the beginning of the Age of Reason (or as Robert Graves has called it, "The Age of Obsequiousness"). He wrote that Donne "perplexes the Minds of the Fair Sex with nice [meaning something like 'minutely argued'] speculations of Philosophy." In other words, Donne was too difficult for the young ladies in whom, Dryden goes on to say, it is the duty of poetry to develop "Sentiment" – i.e., not to bother their pretty young heads with thought. But the implication is that the 'Minds of the Fair Sex' were attracted to Donne's 'Philosophy', enough to perplex themselves with it. Could it be that 'Philosophy', what Dryden is the first to call Donne's "metaphysics", is a red herring here, and that what was really attracting women to Donne was something else? I suspect that what scared Dryden, and necessitated a hatchet job on Donne, was that Donne's early poems were about what we know them to be about – sex. Furthermore, they provoke thought on that dreadful subject.

The *coup de grâce* was dealt by Samuel Johnson some 50 years later (at about the time of *The Gentleman's Magazine*), when he took up Dryden's argument and used the label "metaphysical" for Donne and his successors. The word means 'beyond the physical', and in philosophy 'metaphysics' means the discussion of totally abstract issues – something which never interested Donne. Johnson's grounds for the label were the grotesqueness and intellectual extravagance of the conceits these poets used. They took off from physical reality, as it were. So Donne – the most physical of poets, whose interest was in natural philosophy (science) not speculative, the first person writing in English to use the word 'sex' as we use it now – was granted his place in the literary histories as the first of 'the metaphysicals'. At least it enables young ladies and gentlemen to read his poetry while pretending it is not what it is – that it is, in fact, the reverse. The fiction of the 'metaphysical poets' is still perpetuated in schools. It can at least reassure parents who might be bothered to know that their sons and daughters are reading poetry in which a man frankly compares the vagina of his beloved, her "best lov'd part", with that of his friend's current whore, which is like "the dread mouth of a fired gunne".

Even in Donne's prose, (which can be read as a sort of diffuse and extended discussion of questions he addressed more compactly in his poetry), he reveals a mind which is extraordinarily physical and down to earth – anything but metaphysical. In his sermons, after he had become a 'Doctor' and repudiated his poems, when he bangs on about the resurrection of the dead, he is talking about bodily resurrection. His vision of the Last Judgement is as physical as the 20th century painter Stanley Spencer's depiction of the resurrection in

86

Cookham churchyard, with the lumpy villagers heaving aside their gravestones to clamber out and slap each other on the back.

Jonson's remark about Donne perishing for want of understanding was therefore prophetic, insofar as he has been systematically misrepresented, in a deliberate effort (it is not necessary to assume in Freudian terms that it is 'unconscious': on the contrary it is very conscious) on the part of frightened men (not, though, the women whom they imagine they are protecting) who cannot deal with the fact that his poems think – deeply – about sex.

Jonson's other main point was that Donne had written "all his best pieces err he was 25 years old." That would mean, before 1597. The chronology of Donne's poems is not clear, but as we know it, even some of the *Elegies*, possibly one or two of the *Satires*, and many of the *Songs and Sonets* were written in the 10 years or so following this date. 1607, however, when Donne was 35, is more of a watershed: in that year he was offered an immediate position in the church if he wished to become ordained as a priest. He refused, and was not ordained until 1615. But his life from 1607 onwards was dominated by his progress (a zigzag one) towards the Church. (Before 1607 he had been studying theology, but not yet with a Church career in mind.) Most of the divine sonnets, and 'Mummy', were written by 1608. Allowing Jonson a decade of exaggeration (or perhaps a mishearing by Drummond), "25 years old" can stand in for 35 or 36. Certainly it would be poems written before about this age that Donne would have wanted, later, to seek out and destroy.

There is nothing wrong with being an 'ex-poet'. (The idea is accepted matter-of-factly in the ancient Irish poems of Liadan and Cuirithir). Donne, no doubt, eventually thought of himself as such. But his early poems, fortunately, are not 'ex-poems'. He did not succeed in destroying them.

It is unlikely that Ben Jonson, when reading Donne's early poems, the ones he did like, would have found Donne's language, his allusions, his knotty syntax, his extended conceits, his witticisms, his statements of paradox, his epigrammatic observations – much as all these demand concentrated attention – difficult to understand. It is more likely that he could not always follow Donne's meaning, in that Donne was saying things which went beyond Jonson's own experience and thoughts: that Donne's vision of the world, rather than the way he expressed it, was too radical, too new.

But it is Donne's vision which has appealed to the 20th and 21st centuries. Why? Not because of its religious content, surely, in this age. Mainly because – as any student intuitively knows – of its sexual content. This is why he did in fact perish "for not being understood". He came alive again after 300 years when the intellectual climate permitted readers to face the sexual aspect of his poems and read them as they are – physical, not metaphysical.

Robert Graves, who had a fastidious thing about 'the physical' which put tension into his own poems, sidestepped Donne's vision of sex by referring to Donne's "impersonality". But Donne's very personal tone is echoed in some of Graves' own poems. ("Let us not deny/ The thing's impossibility") It would be hard to name any poet (or pseudo-poet) in English since 1920 or so who has not been influenced by Donne's way of writing about sex and love. Even not in English: the great Scottish Gaelic poet, Sorley MacLean (whose tutor in English Literature at Edinburgh was Grierson), has in his own language and voice absorbed Donne more than most.

Catherine Ing, in *Elizabethan Lyrics,* provided a clear account of what the relation between poetry and criticism was in Donne's own day. She quotes the famous beginning of Puttenham's *Of Poets and Poesie:* "A poet is as much to say as a maker ... Such as (by way of resemblance and reverently) we may say of God." Critics were not professors of English (which was not studied at universities until the late 19th century), they were either poets or readers (both unpaid, it is hardly necessary to add) who took the trouble to record their views in letters, statements which friends wrote down, or treatises such as Puttenham's. As Ing puts it, they tended to "go to two extremes: to the discussion of the general nature of poetry and its place in the world, on the one hand, and to the eager investigation of minute details of prosody on the other." They took the divine nature of the poet's inspiration for granted – that is, they knew that true poetry was not something fabricated, but something that sprang direct out of somewhere, possibly the poet ("'Fool', said my muse to me, 'Look in thy heart and write'", as Philip Sidney put it), possibly not (Donne in 'The Triple Fool' castigated himself for being compelled into writing "whining poetry" which he would have preferred not to write). But whether a (temporarily) divine Maker, or a victim-like Fool, the poet was expected to put much thought and work into the results of his inspiration (or hers – though this was rare unless a woman of huge status like Elizabeth I permitted herself to utter a verse or two) – into craft.

Ing is content to follow the example of the Elizabethan critics, and to discuss craft. Other academic critics, such as Grierson, Helen Gardner, and Theodore Redpath, have contributed to the understanding of Donne, by explicating his texts. Still others, such as R.C. Bald and John Carey, have provided biography and intellectual biography. Insofar as these critics take a historical approach, there is the advantage for the reader that he or she is left to form his or her own views about what Donne's poems actually say. Once the craft, as it were, is explicated (something is learned about Donne's context, his use of words, the sound of his verse), the inspiration can have its way: the reader's emotional response can be the more intense. And as Sorley MacLean has pointed out in an essay on realism in Gaelic poetry, in contrast to what many may believe about emotion somehow vitiating intellect, the more intense the emotion, the more likely a poem is to be realistic. Donne's poetry is a prime example of this: if the reader has done some preliminary work with its language, and is prepared to concentrate, it moves not only the heart but the mind.

Unfortunately, along with almost every other writer ever published, Donne has become a victim of the late 20th century advance of academic criticism into much more ambitious terrain than the intelligent, even loving, explication of a poet's meanings. Criticism has become a subsidised industry and, like other industries, greedy for raw material – either new writers (the thousands of modern novelists and supposed poets can hardly keep up with the necessary production), or new approaches to old ones. But since few critics are gifted enough to take a genuinely new approach, most adopt ready made approaches from the prevailing ideology, and become the bullying Brownshirts, Red Guards, or Thought Police of various intellectual 'isms'. The main current 'isms' are feminism and deconstructionism, but they have sprouted, respectively, from the corpses of Marxism and Freudianism – or in some exponents from a holier-than-thou mixture of the two.

Whatever the critical 'ism', it carries a license to kill, in the form of unrestricted and grandiose interpretation. Donne's poetry has been done over from the usual angles. Two of these interpretations are worth a brief discussion here, because each typifies an ideological approach and each has the net effect of reducing Donne to something he is not, and of turning readers away from him.

The first is Thomas Docherty's *John Donne Undone*. The title is a reference to Donne's poignant note "John Donne, Ann Donne, Undone", and assuming a normal sensitivity to language in Docherty it expresses a wish to 'undo', that is not only to 'deconstruct' (although his approach has been described as "post-deconstructionist") Donne's poems but to destroy him. Docherty's stated goal is a "symptomatic reading or investigation of a psychology" and to elucidate Donne's "masculinist epistemology". Docherty reads Donne's texts closely, but puts in more than he takes out. For example, he compares the flea, in 'The Flea' , on the one hand to a telescope and on the other to a penis. This is partly on the ground that the flea "sucks", and the Elizabethan way of writing the letter 's' resembles an 'f'. This has indeed been played with as a joke for centuries, and it is not hard to imagine that Shakespeare might have enjoyed writing "Where the bee sucks, there suck I" in this double sense. The fact that in poetry, all possible meanings of words tend to operate, on many levels at once, makes this a fair game. But the corollary to meaning in poetry being multi-layered is that it is consistent with itself: this is how a poem tells the truth. And the main message of Donne's poem is that within the flea's "walls of jet", there are three bloods mixing (his, his beloved's, and the flea's – the flea is a Trinity, in fact, like God). Since there is no way in which three bloods are mixed in a penis, Docherty's interpretation cannot work. It nevertheless leads to moralistic peroration: "Donne's self-satisfying predictions in 'The Flea', for example, contrive to translate his own weak auctoritas into the status of the all powerful Logos ...", etc. Since there is no evidence in Donne's own words for such conclusions, and Docherty is interpreting his own interpretations in an infinite regression, it seems reasonable to turn one of the deconstructionists' (and post-deconstructionists') own weapons – pseudo-psychoanalysis – against them here, and suggest that there is some projection at work, and the "weak auctoritas" is the critic's when faced with the poet's "Logos". But how boring all this is, compared to Donne's poem!

The second is Stevie Davies' *John Donne,* which is not boring, and energetically unafraid of tackling what Donne has to say about sex. However, she concludes from a feminist perspective that "Contempt for women remains a major theme of the *Songs and*

Sonets". Now this contains a half-truth, in that Donne is aware of his own tendency to lash out and put women down. The most loving of men or women may feel or express contempt for the other sex at times. Donne is only honest about this, as about most things. (His poems would not be poems if he were not honest at least in them). And given his honesty, and the fact that he is a man, it is hard not to agree with Stevie Davies' statement that "some of the profundity of the *Songs and Sonets* comes of their acknowledgement of those primitive and irrational terrors of woman which nourish, on the one hand, violent and insulting male attitudes and, on the other, insecurity, dependence, and possessiveness." All this can be argued, although a man might come back with the caveat that women too can be violent, insulting, insecure, dependent and possessive. As e.e. cummings concluded a no doubt frightened poem about sexual climax: "C-c-come, said he/ Ummm said she/ Divine! said he./ You are mine, said she".

Stevie Davies goes over the top into what apparently is her 'ism', when she stops discussing Donne's text and asks rhetorically, "Why then should women readers come to Donne at all?" She then 'saves her phenomenon', as the French say, by quoting another critic, Parfitt, saying that Donne's poetry "may be of value to women because it is so revealing of the male." But this male, Donne, in Davies' study is "phallocentric", "obscene", "racist", "gross", "homo-erotic", and prone to "auto-voyeurism", "misogyny", "self-delighting fantasy", etc. Davies seems to enjoy, or at least be stimulated by, Donne's poetry, but her language risks writing him off. Why indeed "should women readers come to Donne at all", if he is all these things? He even, apparently three hundred years ahead of himself, writes a 'sequence' in the elegy 'Going to Bed' which "condemns [sic] feminist objection as prudish and dull-witted." Some of Donne's modern male critics (though not Docherty) come in for the same tarring by Davies. The hapless John Carey – who is still so much under the spell of the 'metaphysical' idea that he states against all the evidence of Donne's poems that he "isn't a love poet at all", "the physical characteristics of the girl ... don't concern him", and "he doesn't even seem to feel sexually excited" – is "macho" and prone to "swashbuckling phallicism"!

In its own way, the criticism of the late 20th century, in which the vigilant ideologue scrutinises a text for evidence of aberration, is as damaging as the nauseating moralism of Dryden, eager to protect young ladies from their own minds. Donne's poetry, which has the net result of freeing intense emotion and thought about what are, even now, unspeakable matters, may be headed for another period of obscurity. It will become shocking again. But since people do not like admitting to being shocked they will dismiss it, as they did to Coleridge and Lamb, as 'a bore'. Its few readers will be left to enjoy it in private, alone or together.

It will not be the first time Donne's poetry has gone underground, as it were. Poetry (apparently safer on the printed page than out on the streets, where in any case it would be taken over by prose) is subversive – Donne's above all.

Select Bibliography

Works by Donne

Donne: Poeticial Works Edited by H.J.C. Grierson. (Oxford, 1929). The irreplaceable standard.

Complete English Poems Edited by C.A. Patrides, revised by R. Hamilton. (Everyman, Dent, 1994). Perhaps the best of the paperback editions, because in the original spelling (although Patrides admits to having occasionally tinkered with the punctuation), and with extensive notes and bibliography.

Complete English Poems Edited by A.J. Smith. (Penguin, 1971). Another comprehensive paperback edition, but blighted by the fact that the spelling is modernized. This is completely unnecessary: any reader of Donne will become used to the original spelling very quickly, and it is essential to the flavour of Donne's writing and his age, as well as to the perception of puns and word-play.

The Songs & Sonets of John Donne Edited by Theodore Redpath. (Methuen, 1983). Irritating on two counts: Redpath's obsession with mix-and-match influence tracing, and modernized spelling. Otherwise, a thorough discussion of background and text.

The Divine Poems Edited by Helen Gardner. (2nd Edition, 1978). Indispensable edition, hard to fault in scholarship or judgement.

Selected Prose Edited by Neil Rhodes. (Penguin, 1987). Excellent selection, very comprehensively edited, in original spelling. But it omits *Ignatius his Conclave*.

Donne's Life

John Donne. A Life R.C. Bald. (Oxford, 1970). The standard biography and source book. Unavoidable. But Bald shows little understanding of poetry, or even interest in it, and Donne's love life seems to leave him cold: with the excuse of avoiding speculation, he avoids consideration of emotion or psychology. But he is willing enough to divagate ad infinitum on the minutiae of ecclesiastical politics.

John Donne. Life, Mind and Art John Carey. (Oxford, 1981). The truth of any statement Carey makes about Donne's poetry can be derived by intellectually reversing it: he is always 180 degrees wrong. However he is always stimulating, and his book is indispensable for an understanding of Donne's religious and intellectual background.

John Donne and his World Derek Parker. (Thames and Hudson, 1975). Modest in scope compared to the two above. Well illustrated, well written, but not always well reasoned. (e.g. "Donne looks at life in a manner which Eliot and Pound made familiar to us in the 1920s.") Connections are assumed between poems and Donne's life which may or may not be true, but no evidence is presented.

John Donne. The Critical Heritage A.J.M. Smith. (Routledge and Kegan Paul: London, 1975). An indispensable compendium of critical and other comments on Donne, from during his lifetime until the mid 20th century.

Note: There are many critical books and essays on Donne, including those by Stevie Davies *(John Donne,* 1994) and T. Docherty *(John Donne, Undone,* 1986). All critical studies are ephemeral, something like journalism, even if they are fun. (Too often, they are not.) They redeem themselves perhaps (as this book attempts to) the more they stay close to the poems and the life, and the more they risk making connections. But modern critical essays will surely date in a few decades, as J.B. Leishmann's *Monarch of Wit,* the standard 30 years ago, has certainly done. Comments on poets which do not date are often (not always) made by other poets. Jonson's and Coleridge's comments on Donne are still of interest. Martin Seymour-Smith's essay in *Poets Through Their Letters* is worth study.

GREENWICH EXCHANGE BOOKS

Greenwich Exchange Student Guides are critical studies of major or contemporary serious writers in English and selected European languages. The series is for the student, the teacher and 'common readers' and is an ideal resource for libraries. The *Times Educational Supplement* (*TES*) praised these books, saying, "The style of these guides has a pressure of meaning behind it. Students should learn from that ... If art is about selection, perception and taste, then this is it."

(ISBN prefix 1-871551- applies)
The series includes:
W.H. Auden by Stephen Wade (-36-6)
Honoré de Balzac by Wendy Mercer (48-X)
William Blake by Peter Davies (-27-7)
The Brontës by Peter Davies (-24-2)
Samuel Taylor Coleridge by Andrew Keanie (-64-1)
Joseph Conrad by Martin Seymour-Smith (-18-8)
William Cowper by Michael Thorn (-25-0)
Charles Dickens by Robert Giddings (-26-9)
John Donne by Sean Haldane (-23-4)
Thomas Hardy by Sean Haldane (-35-1)
Seamus Heaney by Warren Hope (-37-4)
Philip Larkin by Warren Hope (-35-8)
Laughter in the Dark – The Plays of Joe Orton by Arthur Burke (56-0)
Philip Roth by Paul McDonald (72-2)
Shakespeare's Non-Dramatic Poetry by Martin Seymour-Smith (22-6)
Shakespeare's Sonnets by Martin Seymour Smith (38-2)
Tobias Smollett by Robert Giddings (-21-8)
Alfred Lord Tennyson by Michael Thorn (-20-X)
William Wordsworth by Andrew Keanie (57-9)

OTHER GREENWICH EXCHANGE BOOKS
Paperback unless otherwise stated.

Shakespeare's Sonnets
Martin Seymour-Smith
Martin Seymour-Smith's outstanding achievement lies in the field of literary biography and criticism. In 1963 he produced his comprehensive edition, in the old spelling, of *Shakespeare's Sonnets* (here revised and corrected by himself and Peter Davies in 1998). With its landmark introduction and its brilliant critical commentary on each sonnet, it was praised by William

Empson and John Dover Wilson. Stephen Spender said of him "I greatly admire Martin Seymour-Smith for the independence of his views and the great interest of his mind"; and both Robert Graves and Anthony Burgess described him as the leading critic of his time. His exegesis of the *Sonnets* remains unsurpassed.

2001 • 194 pages • ISBN 1-871551-38-2

English Language Skills
Vera Hughes
If you want to be sure, as a student, or in your business or personal life,) that your written English is correct, this book is for you. Vera Hughes' aim is to help you remember the basic rules of spelling, grammar and punctuation. 'Noun', 'verb', 'subject', 'object' and 'adjective' are the only technical terms used. The book teaches the clear, accurate English required by the business and office world. It coaches acceptable current usage and makes the rules easier to remember.
Vera Hughes was a civil servant and is a trainer and author of training manuals.

2002 • 142 pages • ISBN 1-871551-60-9

LITERARY CRITICISM
The Author, the Book and the Reader
Robert Giddings
This collection of essays analyses the effects of changing technology and the attendant commercial pressures on literary styles and subject matter. Authors covered include Charles Dickens, Tobias George Smollett, Mark Twain, Dr Johnson and John le Carré.

1991 • 220 pages • illustrated • ISBN 1-871551-01-3

Liar! Liar!: Jack Kerouac – Novelist
R.J. Ellis
The fullest study of Jack Kerouac's fiction to date. It is the first book to devote an individual chapter to every one of his novels. *On the Road*, *Visions of Cody* and *The Subterraneans* are reread in-depth, in a new and exciting way. *Visions of Gerard* and *Doctor Sax* are also strikingly reinterpreted, as are other daringly innovative writings, like 'The Railroad Earth' and his "try at a spontaneous *Finnegan's Wake*" – *Old Angel Midnight*. Neglected writings, such as *Tristessa* and *Big Sur*, are also analysed, alongside better-known novels such as *Dharma Bums* and *Desolation Angels*.
R.J. Ellis is Senior Lecturer in English at Nottingham Trent University.

1999 • 295 pages • ISBN 1-871551-53-6

BIOGRAPHY
The Good That We Do
John Lucas

John Lucas' book blends fiction, biography and social history in order to tell the story of his grandfather, Horace Kelly. Headteacher of a succession of elementary schools in impoverished areas of London, 'Hod' Kelly was also a keen cricketer, a devotee of the music hall, and included among his friends the great Trade Union leader, Ernest Bevin. In telling the story of his life, Lucas has provided a fascinating range of insights into the lives of ordinary Londoners from the First World War until the outbreak of the Second World War. Threaded throughout is an account of such people's hunger for education, and of the different ways government, church and educational officialdom ministered to that hunger. *The Good That We Do* is both a study of one man and of a period when England changed, drastically and forever.

John Lucas is Professor of English at Nottingham Trent University and is a poet and critic.

2001 • 214 pages • ISBN 1-871551-54-4

In Pursuit of Lewis Carroll
Raphael Shaberman

Sherlock Holmes and the author uncover new evidence in their investigations into the mysterious life and writing of Lewis Carroll. They examine published works by Carroll that have been overlooked by previous commentators. A newly discovered poem, almost certainly by Carroll, is published here.

Amongst many aspects of Carroll's highly complex personality, this book explores his relationship with his parents, numerous child friends, and the formidable Mrs Liddell, mother of the immortal Alice. Raphael Shaberman was a founder member of the Lewis Carroll Society and a teacher of autistic children.

1994 • 118 pages • illustrated • ISBN 1-871551-13-7

Musical Offering
Yolanthe Leigh

In a series of vivid sketches, anecdotes and reflections, Yolanthe Leigh tells the story of her growing up in the Poland of the 30s and the Second World War. These are poignant episodes of a child's first encounters with both the enchantments and the cruelties of the world; and from a later time, stark memories of the brutality of the Nazi invasion, and the hardships of student life in Warsaw under the Occupation. But most of all this is a record of inward development; passages of remarkable intensity and simplicity describe the girl's response to religion, to music, and to her discovery of philosophy.

Yolanthe Leigh was formerly a Lecturer in Philosophy at Reading University.
2000 • 57 pages • ISBN: 1-871551-46-3

Norman Cameron
Warren Hope
Norman Cameron's poetry was admired by W.H. Auden, celebrated by Dylan Thomas and valued by Robert Graves. He was described by Martin Seymour-Smith as, "one of ... the most rewarding and pure poets of his generation ..." and is at last given a full length biography. This eminently sociable man, who had periods of darkness and despair, wrote little poetry by comparison with others of his time, but always of a consistently high quality – imaginative and profound.
2000 • 221 pages • illustrated • ISBN 1-871551-05-6

POETRY
Adam's Thoughts in Winter
Warren Hope
Warren Hope's poems have appeared from time to time in a number of literary periodicals, pamphlets and anthologies on both sides of the Atlantic. They appeal to lovers of poetry everywhere. His poems are brief, clear, frequently lyrical, characterised by wit, but often distinguished by tenderness. The poems gathered in this first book-length collection counter the brutalising ethos of contemporary life, speaking of and for the virtues of modesty, honesty and gentleness in an individual, memorable way.
2000 • 47 pages • ISBN 1-871551-40-4

Baudelaire: Les Fleurs du Mal
Translated by F.W. Leakey
Selected poems from *Les Fleurs du Mal* are translated with parallel French texts and are designed to be read with pleasure by readers who have no French as well as those who are practised in the French language.

F.W. Leakey was Professor of French in the University of London. As a scholar, critic and teacher he specialised in the work of Baudelaire for 50 years and published a number of books on the poet.
2001 • 153 pages • ISBN 1-871551-10-2

Lines from the Stone Age
Sean Haldane
Reviewing Sean Haldane's 1992 volume *Desire in Belfast*, Robert Nye wrote in *The Times* that "Haldane can be sure of his place among the English

poets." This place is not yet a conspicuous one, mainly because his early volumes appeared in Canada and because he has earned his living by other means than literature. Despite this, his poems have always had their circle of readers. The 60 previously unpublished poems of *Lines from the Stone Age* – "lines of longing, terror, pride, lust and pain" – may widen this circle.
2000 • 53 pages • ISBN 1-871551-39-0

Wilderness
Martin Seymour-Smith
This is Martin Seymour-Smith's first publication of his poetry for more than 20 years. This collection of 36 poems is a fearless account of an inner life of love, frustration, guilt, laughter and the celebration of others. He is best known to the general public as the author of the controversial and bestselling *Hardy* (1994).
1994 • 52 pages • ISBN 1-871551-08-0